THE POWER TO SEE IT THROUGH

Jim McGuiggan

International Biblical Resources
5101 2nd St., Lubbock, TX 79416

5101 2nd St.
Lubbock, TX 79416

ISBN 0-932397-20-4

Cover Design and Art Work By
Van and Ronelle Howell

2014

With Love +
Spiritual Growth
In Christian Love
Michelle

To my precious brother,
Eddie
Quick to laugh,
always encouraging,
conscientious and God-centered.
And to his wife,
Margaret
Devoted Christian,
wife, mother
and friend.

Contents

Foreword

There are those who go through life with a smile. Never seeming to have a crisis of faith or a difficulty that silences them. Thank God for them! They know where their strength lies!

There are those who narrow their lives, who refuse to shoulder burdens, who carry only as much as they choose for only as long as they choose it. Life is a happy-go-lucky journey. They show no burdened heart because they refuse to have one. They are "innoculated" with a weak strain of the "Christian virus" and never experience the full impact of the "disease." They wish Christ well in his fine plans and purposes for the world, they hope he'll win, and like Tito in George Eliot's *Romola*, they are quite prepared to make any sacrifice just so long as it isn't too inconvenient. They make it the aim of their life to avoid involvement and passion for these only lead to pain.

This little book is geared for those who are wrestling with the war and trouble Christ brings into a life that seeks devotion to him. It has nothing to say to those who know no struggle or to those who are prepared to stand back and let others bear the heat of battle unaided. It is written for the wounded and for those who regard it as a part of living to be helpers of the wounded.

Introduction

Why Do So Many Fail To See It Through?

Some of them are worn down by life's endless struggle. It's easy for richly blessed people to think they would be as noble and as devoted to God as they now are even if they had not been richly blessed. But take away from us our wonderful families, our loving friends, our Sunday school teachers, our decent jobs—take from us all these lovely things and have us born in some soul-killing ghetto, what then?

There's no point in dismissing this by saying that lots of people have beaten a horrible, life-long environment. Of course that's true! But we point to such people because they are remarkable—they aren't the norm! Most children born and raised in corruption are destroyed by it. When we come across some who have joyously risen above all that, we're thrilled and inspired by it. The opposite is also true!

Take a child raised in a godly, loving, well-balanced home. Give him good health, good food and pleasant surroundings. Let him see his parents loving and respecting one another, give him good schooling and warm upright friends. Now, see him pursue shameful and criminal things. Aren't we shocked?! Don't we shake our heads in wonder. "You'd think with such advantages in life he would turn out better!" we murmur. And we're right to be puzzled! We expect this ideal environment to result in a noble and upright young man. When it doesn't, we're perplexed. Environment isn't all-powerful, but it's very powerful! It wears people down or it raises them up. If a godly and loving home, richly blessed is an *advantage*, why isn't an ungodly, hate-filled and impoverished home a *disadvantage*?

Life's inequalities can wear people down! In Exodus 6:9, the Israelites couldn't listen well to Moses because of the pain of their environment. They were beaten down by cruel bondage and discouragement!

Alice lived two houses from us more than twenty-five years ago. She wasn't a Christian, and those of us who knew her well knew that she had inner struggles she didn't always win. But Christ loved her! And, Christian or not, he worked in her life, making her cheerful, sensitive and sharing. Like so many others she had a hard life. She had four kids, serious heart trouble and a hard-drinking husband who beat her when he felt like it (and he felt like it regularly).

I can still see her in the street, leaning against the wall by her window with arms folded, wisecracking with some passing neighbors. More than once I caught her crying, wondering how she was going to get through the week with so little money and so many things to be done with it. She was thin, too thin, but her skin was so clear and smooth, almost transparent, and her eyes were beautiful—pale blue and big and round. She died undergoing her second heart surgery. I think she was thirty-two!

Alice reminds me of all the people I know who, day after day, *without end*, struggle to keep their heads above water. *Never* in all their lives are they able to go to a shop and buy something without first doing some serious arithmetic! *Never*, from the cradle to the grave, are they *sure* the money for the rent, heat, food and clothing is going to be there. It's that endless grind that beats so many people. That's what takes the light out of their eyes. They march up from the gates of birth with the sunshine of hope on their faces, dreaming dreams and making plans, but life just wears them down. And then we put them into the ground at *thirty-two*, sadly look at each other and shrug in helplessness!

He had lost his adoring wife and just couldn't seem to get over it. "It was the morning," he said, almost to himself, "the terrible mornings when one cried out, 'Not yet! O God, not yet! Have I another whole long day of it to face so soon.' " And it's *right*, but it isn't *enough* to say: "Get hold of yourself! You've got to shake yourself out of it!" Nor does it make a lot of difference to *him* that others have been through the same pain and won. He isn't them! And some of them are crushed, forever!

Many are worn out by the struggle against sin. Gossip said,

> Those who fail in religion [most often] do so . . . through sheer depression and a daunted feeling that it has proved to be of no use in their case at least. . . . things turn out not at all what they had expected: they had supposed that one pitched battle would bring matters to a decisive issue, and that thereafter there would be little more to do than the hunting down of broken groups of disheartened failings. . . . that, and the procession through the cheering street, and it is with dismay that they waken up to discover that they are immersed in a prolonged campaign of dull trench warfare, in which from day to day not much that is vital seems to happen, until growing heartsick of the mud and the shelling . . . and the brave rushes that appear to make no real difference . . . . they make a kind of dishonorable peace

> and slink off home. Or things go wrong more tragically, and they fling down their weapons, surrender to themselves, stop trying, assume hopelessly that nothing further can be done, and let the fierce currents of their nature drift them where they will. That's how souls go down!

Many come to believe that God can't really love them. David, in Psalm 8, wondered why God bothered with puny man. What would he have thought if he could see the universe through our modern telescopes? Have you never staggered at the thought of Someone so powerful, wanting to deal with us at all? *Never?*

What of the suffering we see going on in the world? The rape of whole nations, the exploitation of the masses, the abuse of children, the success crime seems to enjoy, the muggings of the elderly and the stench of the housing complexes where greedy landlords have the people boxed in like so many animals in a pen? Has this never assaulted your mind and made you to wonder? Would it surprise you if people living under those conditions had occasional doubts about the love of God?

But it appears to me that many have their first doubts about God's love for them when they look at their sinfulness! Either their lives appear to be pathetic and trivial, or their struggle with the grosser evils appear to be a losing one. In either case they begin to wonder how a holy God could stomach them. They can hardly face themselves so, they feel, an infinitely holy God must find them unbearably evil or trivial. And if you add to this the speed with which the friends of God (Christians) seem to tire of them should their struggle against sin not progress as well as the Christians think it should, the doubts grow stronger.

Many are bored listless by the lack of challenge or relevancy in the Christ they hear proclaimed week after week. A Catholic priest once said: If the Protestant pulpit is ever to die it will be found stabbed to death in some alley with a Protestant sermon sticking in its back. Whether or not that's fair criticism, the Christ we see is the Christ the minister brings to us in weekly sermons. Depending on how he feels, we get one portrait of Christ or another.

The central issues in so much preaching is *church attendance* and financial *contributions*. There is so much competition between churches and so many reputations on the line based on *church growth* and *numbers*. Where this is the case, the "weekly bulletins from the Almighty" have large doses of "Let's bring our friends," "Let's have an attendance drive" or "Let's meet the budget the leaders have set." A steady diet of this, and the heart and soul of the people begins to grow thin and weary. Joy in the presence of God on a daily basis is gradually replaced with "doing your part" in bolstering the numbers of the local assembly and attending without fail even the midweek meetings.

In many assemblies there is no big push for numbers; there is the constant chorus of "how right we are and how wrong everyone else is." For a while that may act as a support for the soul of those who love truth, but it soon becomes a meatless bone. A God who is always and only interested in people holding correct views and exposing those who don't (even if the "heretic's" lifestyle is glorious), a God like that loses attractiveness and has little to say about *life*. He's always talking to people who aren't at the assembly, that is, the people "out there" who hold all these errors the preacher is telling us about. And since there's more to life than being "correct" about every verse of Scripture you read, many people grow listless and weary with the God they've been led to believe has nothing to say about *life* as a whole.

Then there are the churches which ask nothing of anyone. They are all "nice" people being "nice" one to another; as someone put it, it's "the bland leading the bland." The church becomes a club with "nice" social overtones, where no one is passionate about anything, where there isn't enough drive to produce a heresy much less the recognition of a compelling truth. There are churches where everyone dresses well, succeeds in business, sings hymns if they aren't too "fundamentalist" and, in general, have a happy time as a member of that church. Elmer Suderman bitterly spoke of just such an assembly. He spoke of them as baptized in the smell of classic Chanel, sun-tanned, soft-skinned, "elegant, swellegant, natty, delectable, suave, cool, adorable and *damned*." The psalmist reminds us (Ps. 106:15), that a well-fed and well-dressed people had "leanness" in their soul!

God Loves Losers Too!

Losers lose *in spite of* what God wants for them! If Ezekiel 18:23 and 32 mean anything at all, they mean God feels awful pain when losers lose. Love *involves* a desire to see justice done, so God must punish oppressors and rebels, but if we think God is a "heavenly hit man" who enjoys his work, we haven't begun to know him!

Matthew 23 is one of the most scathing pieces in literature, but it doesn't end with: "Woe . . . hypocrites . . . sons of hell!" It ends with a heartbroken Christ saying he felt like a mother hen in panic, desperately wanting to hide her chicks under her wings because danger is near.

Luke 15 makes it very clear that when sinners lose, God loses too. No shepherd sought a lost sheep more fervently than God pursues lost people! No finder is more thrilled as he joyously walks home with a lamb on his shoulders than God is when he holds a former wanderer close to his heart (out of which the wanderer had never wandered however far he had wandered).

The God who has uniquely revealed himself in Jesus Christ is *for* us. If he came at all, he came to do us good! If he came to serve, he came to serve the selfish, for that's what we are. If he came to die, he came to die for destroyers of life, for that's what we are. If he came to offer friendship and reconciliation, he came to offer it to treacherous people, for that's what we are.

We're going to have to make up our minds to this, God thinks us precious. He thinks it worthwhile to redeem us at awful cost. In Romans 5:6-10 we're assured that he died for the weak and ungodly (v. 6), for the sinner (v. 8) and for the enemies (v. 10). And can God who *so* loved us, rejoice when we eternally lose?

We read of a father who's worth millions and lives in the lap of luxury. His boy is wayward and far from home. The father is fragmented, lonely, and he lives oblivious to all his vast wealth. That doesn't surprise us, does it? We know of a mother who is honored by the community, the state, maybe even the nation. Her daughter lives in shameful rebellion in some squalid hut, away from the mother who adores her. Does it surprise us that the mother finds no lasting joy in the recognition she receives? She'd gladly swap it all for the love and blessing of her foolish daughter. That isn't hard for us to believe! We know of friends, brothers, sisters who gladly give themselves one for another, who compete, it appears, to outdo one another in expressions of genuine love and affection. We see all this, and *because we believe it, we are warmed and moved by it.*

We can believe that sinners can give their children bread rather than stones; we can accept fully that a father can give his son fish rather than a serpent—but we find it hard to believe God can outdo sinners in his love for his creation! Luke 15 says something to us, but never enough. The book of Hosea grabs us by the lapels and looks right into our eyes with its message of God's passionate love for wicked people, urging us: Believe it! Believe it!

Do we think, because our love is shallow, that his is? He has already endured the final insult! He passionately sought the opportunity to embrace the ultimate insult and dishonor! Does that not tell us once and for all that God rejoices in our joy and grieves at our loss? *After the cross, it isn't fair to doubt God!*

But I'm sure it's the holiness of God, his justice, that makes us afraid to lean too heavily on his love toward us. And yet we're explicitly told that God is *just* in forgiving our sins (1 Jn. 1:9). We're expressly told that God shows himself *just* in passing over our sins in view of the death of Christ (Rom. 3:24-26). In the death of Christ a *righteous* God is expressing his love to us. His love isn't immoral. His love doesn't despise justice. But his justice doesn't get in the way of his loving us! Whatever theory of the atonement you subscribe to, it's still true that *in Christ, God pays the price in order to love us!*

We permit our sins to separate us from God even when he assures us that it has been dealt with in Christ Jesus. We live, never free from the notion that God is always on edge, becoming more and more irritable with us. We glance around fearing a smashing blow from his huge fist because we've wronged him again. We see his acts of discipline as proofs of his lovelessness rather than what he has expressly told us they are (Rev. 3:19), expressions of his love toward us. And when we reject him with finality and insist on losing, we feel we're getting what God wanted us to have all along and we feel, since we are now utterly lost, God is content. And God feels again the throb in his hands and feet and head and weeps. *God loses when we lose, and God loves even the losers!*

Where Do People Get The Power To See It Through?

There are no noble thoughts which do not find their ultimate source in God himself! There are no lovely and selfless things done unless God fathers them! No one speaks beautiful and uplifting words that God is not the author of. Every good and perfect thing that Man has or has done comes from God!

Bible believers insist that this is true for all those who wear the name of Christ. They gladly accept the truth Jesus spoke (Jn. 15:5) when he said that apart from him we can do nothing! It is *God* who works in us both to will and do his good pleasure (Phil. 2:13), and it is *he* who works in us that which is well pleasing in his sight (Heb. 13:20-21).

But we believers are often slow to confess that God is at work in the lives of those who haven't yet said *yes* to Jesus. For one reason or another we're reluctant to admit that God ennobles the lives of those who do not acknowledge him. A thoroughly unbiblical notion makes the rounds in religious circles that one must be a Christian in order to experience the ennobling work of the Spirit of God in life. *This isn't true!* From ancient times God has made it clear that he is at work in people who don't know him. One doesn't have to be "indwelt" by the Spirit to produce the kind of fruit the Spirit produces.

Cornelius was already a very godly man indeed before Peter ever came to him to bring him the fullness of truth by which he was saved in Jesus Christ (Acts 10:1-4; 11:13-14). And Lydia, long before she was baptized into Christ was a gloriously lovely lady (Acts 16). All around us, every day of our lives, we watch people endure torment with a nobility that stuns us. Where do we think they get such strength? How often have you heard people say their neighbors who aren't Christians show more integrity than some who are? Are we amazed that a Samaritan heretic returned to thank Christ for healing when nine orthodox believers didn't? Christ wasn't amazed at it; he was saddened by it. And when he turned in amazement at the greatness of the centurion's faith (Lk. 7), aren't we being told that God operates in the lives of people outside our "fold"? (The ancient Jews found this idea offensive. God was going to use Cyrus, the heathen, to redeem Israel from captivity and the Jews didn't like it. See Is. 45:1, 4, 9-13.)

Christians or non-Christians, God gives the strength to live nobly to all the socially useful people we see around us. We will not give the credit to the Devil for the loveliness in the lives of people who have not yet turned to God in Christ! Nor will we deny that such loveliness exists. I've heard people go in that direction. In the end, there's no answering such people. We find adoring husbands, devoted wives, loving and wise parents, loyal friends and respectful children throughout the world who haven't yet said *yes* to Christ as Lord. They may not have made a commitment to him, but he has made a commitment to them. To the degree that any of us is honorable and noble and brave—it has been worked in us by God. Wherever in the world we find people bravely living radiant lives in spite of unspeakable poverty, outrageous oppression and disease-bringing hunger, there, right there, we see God at work! *The power to see it through comes only from God! From nowhere and no one else!*

This truth means that no one can boast! Paul insisted that what he was, he was by the grace of God (1 Cor. 15:10). He insisted that the life he was able to live was because Christ was living in him (Gal. 2:20). And he prodded the smug Corinthians by telling them they had nothing they weren't given, that whatever difference there was between them and others was the work of God, that if they were *given* all their blessings they had no grounds to strut (1 Cor. 4:7).

But how does God go about enabling people? How does he give them the power to see it through? There is no one avenue through which God blesses us with that kind of power. Every thinking person could make up his/her own wise list. To give us the power to see it through God brings us face to face with truths we must acknowledge and people who enrich us in so many ways. What follows are some of the things I think about when I think of people who've been granted the power to see their pilgrimage through in a radiant way.

O God, our Father, our souls are made sick by the sight of hunger and want and nakedness; of little children bearing on their bent backs the burden of the world's work; of motherhood drawn under the grinding wheels of modern industry; and of overburdened manhood, with empty hands, stumbling and falling. Help us to understand that it is not thy purpose to do away with life's struggle, but that thou desirest us to make the conditions of that struggle just and its results fair.

Enable us to know that we may bring this to pass only through love and sympathy and understanding;

only as we realize that all are alike thy children—the rich and the poor, the strong and the weak, the fortunate and the unfortunate. And so, our Father, give us an ever-truer sense of human sisterhood; that with patience and steadfastness we may do our part in ending the injustice that is in the land, so that all may rejoice in the fruits of their toil and be glad in thy sunshine. Keep us in hope and courage even amid the vastness of the undertaking and the slowness of the progress, and sustain us with the knowledge that our times are in thy hand. Amen.

HELEN RING ROBINSON

1

Hope

We are never beneath hope, while above hell; nor above hope, while beneath heaven.

SHAKESPEARE

If the mere delay of hope deferred makes the heart sick, what will the death of hope—its final and total disappointment—despair, do to it?

NEVINS

Let us hold unswervingly to the hope we profess, for he who promised is faithful.

HEBREWS 10:23

The unbeliever insists upon living out of his own resources and so is anxious about his own future in the illusion of being able to dispose over it. . . . The man who is concerned for himself factually lives in fear . . . shutting himself up against a future, which is not at his disposal.

BULTMANN

To talk with God, No breath is lost—
Talk on!
To walk with God, No strength is lost—
Walk on!
To wait on God, No time is lost—
Wait on!

And hope does not disappoint us, because God has poured out his love into our hearts by the Holy Spirit, whom he has given us.

ROMANS 5:5

The People With The Power To See It Through Have . . .

Hope

Bruce Larson says he visited the famous Menninger psychiatric clinic. He asked some of the staff what it was above everything else that made a difference in the treatment and healing of people suffering from serious emotional disorders. That group told him that the whole staff agreed on what the factor was; it was *hope*! They confessed they didn't know how to give people hope but they insisted that they could actually see the change in a person when *hope* arrived!

And what is *hope*? In biblical usage *hope* is a complex word which in some contexts embraces trust and endurance so there's something of an over-simplification in Hoffman's correct definition. He tells us *hope* is never fearful anticipation, "it is the expectation of something good."[1] Bultmann says it is "sure confidence."[2] The man who has *hope* is convinced that something good is going to happen! To have *hope* is to have a future!

Do you know what kills *hope*? Can you list some of the things that are obstacles to *hope*? Here are a few of my own "obstacles to hope."

1. *The tyranny of appearances.* When he's functioning well, the Christian doesn't live by what he can see. He has an "invisible" means of support. He "sees the invisible" (Heb. 11). But Christians, like everyone else, take their eyes off the invisible and begin to weigh the probability of success or failure on what they can see. And when, like Peter, they take their eyes off what they can't see and put them on what they can see, the appearance of things chips away at their confidence. (See Mt. 14:30.)

2. *The strength of the enemy and our feebleness.* When appearance begins to lord it over us, we notice the awful strength of the enemy and our pathetic weaknesses. Entrenched enemies. Enemies with centuries of experience. Enemies with the power of the government behind them. Enemies whose strength grows stronger with each passing generation. Enemies outside of ourselves and enemies within us. "Nothing good can be expected under these circumstances," we mutter to ourselves.

3. *A past littered with personal defeats and failures.* Looking back on our lives we see a host of broken promises, vows we made which we never kept, resolutions made in blood-red earnestness that vanished like snow off a bush when the sun rises. A lifelong wrestling with character flaws that seems only to deepen with the passing years. We've read books, attended seminars, listened to tapes, prayed prayers and shed tears without any real progress being made. "Things will never get better!" we murmur in our weariness.

4. *A trail of broken promises and deserting friends.* But we aren't the only ones to make promises. Others told us they'd be there if we needed them, and they weren't!

Vows were made in the warm days of friendship but were broken when the cooling winds of what the vows would cost began to blow. We found ourselves weak, vulnerable, losing and *alone*. Then we began to wonder if things could ever be any better, until the light of hope went out and we were left drifting along *wishing* but unable to *hope*!

Biblical Hope Is Centered In God and Christ

There aren't many verses more lovely and poignant than Psalm 39:7 which says: "And now, Lord, for what do I wait? My hope is in thee" (RSV).

Life is confusing to David. It's too brief! It doesn't seem to have purpose! It doesn't satisfy! A man may accomplish much and may even become very wealthy, but what's the point of it all? No matter how great a kingdom he builds, no matter what he accomplishes, he feels like a paper plate or a plastic fork—useless after being used. David has the questions burning inside him but he doesn't want to speak in case it brings reproach on God. Finally, he can't keep quiet any longer. So he speaks to God alone. Listen to this: "I said, 'I will guard my ways, that I may not sin with my tongue; I will bridle my mouth, so long as the wicked are in my presence.' I was dumb and silent, I held my peace to no avail; my distress grew worse, my heart became hot within me. As I mused, the fire burned; then I spoke with my tongue: . . ." (Ps. 39:1-3; RSV).

The psalmist has only questions, only issues that disturb him. Life doesn't provide the answers for his tormented heart. But instead of letting his doubts be his lord, he doubts his doubts and embraces the God who chastises him, the God who refuses to take away the inner burden by giving cheap answers. Since he can find no answers in a life filled with turmoil and questions, he says: "And now, Lord, for what do I wait? My hope is in thee." Only God can deliver him from his transgressions and his feelings of despondency (Ps. 39:7-13; RSV).

The psalms are full of *hope*, and men are led to *hope* in God and his promises (see a concordance on *hope*). In the New Testament *hope* is centered in God and in Christ in whom God has manifested himself (1 Tim. 1:1; 4:10). And that *hope* is *living* because God is living and because Christ is alive forevermore (1 Pet. 1:3; Rev. 1:18).

Where *hope* is *not* placed in God and Christ, there can be no security in the future. *Hope* is much like biblical trust; it is the surrendering of one's own resources and looking to God for the final and desired outcome.

If we place our *hope* for the future in our skill, wealth, health, education, friends, family, political influence or brilliance, we open ourselves up to fear and uncertainty. What do we do when our health, skill or brilliance vanishes with approaching age? What do we do when we are left behind in the race for new knowledge which means our old knowledge is useful but not enough? What do we do when our friends and family turn up with no hope of their own? Or when our political party falls into disfavor? "The unbeliever," Bultmann rightly says, "insists upon living out of his own resources and so is anxious about his own future in the illusion of being able to dispose over it. . . . The man who is concerned for himself factually lives in fear . . . shutting himself up against a future, which is not at his disposal."[3]

Biblical Hope Never Shames Us (Rom. 5:5)

To *hope* in God and Christ means we believe two big

things are true: (1) God is *able* and (2) God is *faithful.*

God *is* able! Take a moment to leisurely read Isaiah 40 and drink in its message. God is *able*! Of Christ it's said that he is *able* to save for all time those who come to God by him (Heb. 7:25; RSV).

But it isn't God's ability that we doubt, it is his willingness or faithfulness we ponder over. Not that we think God is ever faithless! No, we wrestle about his faithfulness in dealing with us who are often faithless. Will he not turn away from us in disgust? Will his patience run out on us when we make so little progress? Will not our trivial lives and our feebleness cause him to wash his hands of us?

And so our eyes wander from *him* to ourselves! We take the truth that we must cooperate with him, and that truth becomes the only truth, the truth we're obsessed with. We accept the truth that we must pursue his will and likeness and *that* truth becomes the dominant truth of life. In this way we begin to depend again on our own resources! We look to our own possibilities and potential. *This is not the New Testament approach to things!* It, too, teaches us about the need for us to cooperate with God, but the emphasis in the New Testament is on *God's* resources and *God's* faithfulness. Take the next few moments and read these few verses.

> [God] will keep you strong to the end, so that you will be blameless on the day of our Lord Jesus Christ. God, who has called you into fellowship with his Son, Jesus Christ our Lord, is faithful.
>
> (1 Cor. 1:8-9)

> May God himself, the God of peace, sanctify you through and through. May your whole spirit, soul and body be kept blameless at the coming of our Lord Jesus Christ. The one who

> calls you is faithful and he will do it.
> (1 Thess. 5:23-24)

> But the Lord is faithful, and he will strengthen and protect you from the evil one.
> (2 Thess. 3:3)

> So then, those who suffer according to God's will should commit themselves to their faithful Creator and continue to do good.
> (1 Pet. 4:19)

> What if some did not have faith? Will their lack of faith nullify God's faithfulness?
> (Rom. 3:3)

> Resting on the hope of eternal life, which God, who does not lie, promised before the beginning of time.
> (Tit. 1:2)

> Let us hold unswervingly to the hope we profess, for he who promised is faithful.
> (Heb. 10:23)

> If we confess our sins, he is faithful and just and will forgive us our sins and purify us from all unrighteousness.
> (1 Jn. 1:9)

Do you know a man who has always kept his word? Who felt it was a part of right living to fulfill what he promised? A good man, on whom you could rely come what may? Well, when you think of him, hear God saying to you: "I'm like that! You can depend on me! When I give my word, you can be sure that I'll fulfill it!" Such people are God's gift to us, and they remind us of the ever-faithful God who keeps his promises.

Because God is holy, we can *hope* for holiness. "The one

who calls you is faithful and he will do it" (1 Thess. 5:24). Christ's experience with God led him to say: "Thy word is truth" (Jn. 17:17; RSV).

But when we look at our lives, their pathetic, shabby and shallow nature, we're inclinded to murmur that his *promises* are not squaring with the *reality* of things. And we find ourselves restless, shamed, disappointed despite the greatness of our longings and the gallantry of our dreams. But we have the assurance that our noble dreams *will* come to pass because "he who promised is faithful"!

Every dream that haunts us, every vision that shames us, every tremor of revulsion we feel over our meanness that won't let us have peace, every restless longing after decency and gallantry, every chastising stroke that cuts us till we cry out in our anger and our shame *is the work of God in us*! These things are the proof that God is working toward holiness in us. (See Heb. 13:20-21 and Phil. 2:13.)

We mustn't think these noble dreams are ours! That the restless longings are our creation! It is God who is working in us this holy discontent, this shame at our shame, this despising of our meanness! And he who causes us to dream these lovely dreams will bring them to completion because "he who calls us is faithful and he will do it"! Will he who creates beauty not give us the ability to appreciate it? Will he who creates lovely music in man not give him the hearing to take it in? Will he who made the air not give us lungs to breathe it? Will he who created our longing for cleanness and life not fulfill it? Will sinful creatures dream lovely, noble, gallant and decent dreams and fail to reach them only because their God is faithless or feeble?

But I have sinned, you say. Have failed miserably, again and again. I've been treacherous and evil. Yes, and "he is *faithful* and just and will forgive us our sins and purify us from all unrighteousness."

"Write down what it is that you need to be, what in your finest hours you long to be," God urges us, "and I 'will meet all your needs according to [my] glorious riches in Christ Jesus' " (Phil. 4:19). "And when the final chapter is written," he seems to say, "we'll look back over it all and see whether in anything I overestimated what I could do for you, or if there was a single promise I didn't fulfill."

Biblical Hope Is a Gift From God

We aren't wanting to do less for God; we're wanting to do more. We aren't wanting to *be* less for God; we're wanting to be more. We know full well that we are to labor, together *with* God. But our *hope* doesn't lie in our resources; it's based on *his*! And this conviction that "good things are going to happen" is the gift of a gracious God! We can't toil our way to *hope*, we can't earn it, we can't worry our way to it, scheme our way to it or buy it. We receive it as a gracious gift. We say *yes* to God's promise knowing that he is able and faithful. Look at these three passages:

> May the God of hope fill you with all joy and peace as you trust in him, so that you may overflow with hope by the power of the Holy Spirit.
>
> (Rom. 15:13)

> May our Lord Jesus Christ himself and God our Father, who loved us and by his grace gave us eternal encouragement and good hope, encourage your hearts and strengthen you in every good deed and word.
>
> (2 Thess. 2:16-17)

> Remember your word to your servant, for you have given me hope. My comfort in my suffering is this: Your promise preserves my life.
>
> (Ps. 119:49-50)

And this living hope, this vibrant conviction that "good things are going to happen," this radiant assurance that we need not be and we will not always be as we now are, gives power to our struggle! It gives strength to our endurance. The evils around us and within us may look like winners now, but that's how evil looks on Friday, says Campolo's preaching friend—"Sunday's coming!" The resurrection of Jesus Christ creates hope in our hearts (1 Pet. 1:3). We can't be beaten!

On Friday Pilate washed his hands, Herod mocked and Annas showed his malice—but Sunday was coming! The Pharisees grinned, the Sadducees chuckled and the Romans yawned, on Friday—but Sunday was coming! The crowd screamed, Caiaphas strutted and women wept, on Friday—but Sunday was coming! On Friday the demons danced, the Devil rejoiced and soldiers mocked the living Lord—but Sunday was coming! The earth convulsed, the tombs cracked open and the sun pulled down the shade on something unfit to watch, on Friday—but Sunday came around! And *hope* became deathless!

Our pain and our confusion, our guilt and our weariness, all take their toll. But the last word is God's and *that's* why we can overflow with *hope*. In the end, we win! We don't have to ignore the trouble and pain and evil around and within us in order to be optimistic! The darker colors of life need not be ignored! Christ insisted that the two men on the Emmaus road squarely face the unpleasant side of the will of God. No religion that doesn't do that is fit to live! But he also insisted that there was a happy ending despite the unpleasant truths

(Lk. 24:25-27). The cross is to be viewed through the tomb! *Hope thou in God!* (Ps. 42).

Biblical Hope Doesn't Despise Life That Now Is

I've heard people described as "so heavenly minded they are no earthly use." I can easily imagine that some people are so future oriented they can't be bothered trying to make things in this life any better. But that isn't *God's* intention!

No one was more hope-filled than Jesus Christ, and here's how Acts 10:38 summarizes the life of Christ: "God anointed Jesus of Nazareth with the Holy Spirit and power, and . . . he went around doing good and healing all who were under the power of the devil, because God was with him."

The "hope" for the future that makes a man less socially useful is not biblical! The "hope" that leads people to despise earth-life is an offense against the incarnation of God in Jesus Christ. The "hope" that leads a man to laziness or lounging his way through life will be decisively stamped as a fraud at the judgment. "Hope" cannot be biblical if it makes people less like the Christ of Acts 10:38. Because the future holds inexpressibly wonderful things, gives us no reason for denying that God's creation is less than "very good."

All the hopeful men and women of Scripture were socially useful! They served their fellow-humans. Reflect a while on Joseph as he waited to see his dreams fulfilled! Think on Abraham as he hoped against hope! And Paul who gives us a brief glimpse into his tireless work for Christ in 2 Corinthians 11. Hope doesn't paralyze, it inspires; it doesn't blind us to the present though it casts its eye to the future.

Lord God, who gave strength to Abraham to hope against hope for the fulfillment of thy promises, we request of thee that thou wilt bless us, too, with that power. Lift our restless eyes from the things we see, to thee O Lord, the father of hope. Bless us with balance that we may not ask of ourselves what is only thy power to accomplish and that we may not ask of thee to do what we by thy grace must do—trust thee. May our hope, sovereign Lord, be as alive as He is alive and may we recognize that the ground of our hope is thy Fatherhood and His resurrection. Deliver us from the anxiety which comes from depending on our own integrity, and enable us, strong Father, to trust not in our love for thee but in thy love for us. And when the tide of things seems to be running against us, when mocking voices ask where our God is and why we should radiantly look to the future when the earth breaks beneath us, bless us so with thy presence that we may be ready to give a radiant answer concerning the hope that is within us. We pray with confidence for thou art faithful who called us, and you will do it. Amen.

Endnotes

[1]Hoffman, "*elpis*" in *New International Dictionary of New Testament Theology*, ed. Colin Brown (Grand Rapids, Mich.: Zondervan Publishing Co., 1975), 2:241.

[2]Rudolf Bultmann, "*elpis*," in *Theological Dictionary of the New Testament*, ed. Gerhard Kittel, trans. and ed. Geoffrey W. Bromiley (Grand Rapids, Mich.: Wm. B. Eerdmans Publishing Co., 1964), 2:517.

[3]Rudolf Bultmann, *Theology of the New Testament* (New York: Scribner, 1951), 1:320.

2

Suffering

Do you sometimes long for that simple and unquestioning faith in God's love which you had when you knelt at your mother's knee? That you cannot have. God has a better thing in store for you. In the things of love as much as in the things of faith and hope you must put away childish things. God has this message for you, which meets all the breadth of your manhood's thought, and all the depth of your manhood's need.

W. M. CLOW

Paneloux is a man of learning, a scholar. He hasn't come in contact with death; that's why he can speak with such assurance of the truth—with a capital T. But every country priest who visits his parishoners, and has heard a man gasping for breath on his deathbed, thinks as I do. He'd try to relieve human suffering before trying to point out its excellence.

ALBERT CAMUS

One, for example, looking at Calvary, may center his attention on the cross alone, saying, "There can be no good God in a world where such unjust cruelty happens"; or he may center his attention upon the Christ upon the cross, saying, "There must be a good God in a world that produces him."

HARRY E. FOSDICK

There is only one question that really matters: Why do bad things happen to good people?

HAROLD S. KUSHNER

The People With
The Power To See It Through
Have Come To Terms With . . .

Suffering

Harold Kushner said: "There is only one question that really matters: Why do bad things happen to good people? All other theological conversation is intellectually diverting; somewhat like doing the crossword puzzle in the Sunday paper and feeling very satisfied when you have made the words fit. . . . Virtually every meaningful conversation I have ever had with people on the subject of God and religion has either started with this question, or gotten around to it before long." *Maybe* Kushner has exaggerated but it's a pardonable exaggeration.

The people who have the power to see it through have faced the awful reality of suffering without loss of radiant and productive faith.

A Few Preliminary Remarks

I don't think there is a fully satisfying answer to the question: Why does suffering exist in a universe controlled by a good God? Because we aren't simply "logic boxes" or "breathing computers." We find it awfully hard to reason while we're sobbing and lonely.

I think it's past time for the human race to fully accept the direct responsibility for almost all the suffering that has occurred and is occurring in the world rather than blaming it on God.

I think we need to stop thanking God for giving humans free will and at the same time screaming at *him* when people exercise their free will to torment each other.

By far, the bulk of the whole human race refuses to believe that suffering in the world is sufficient reason to "dump" God. Almost always, the people who "dump" God over the "suffering problem" are healthy, well-off philosophers and philosophizers. Those who *know* suffering at close quarters deny the conclusions of the "armchair" sufferers.

The People With the Power To See It Through View Their Agonized Wonderings As Normal and Human

The Bible is full of people who groan out protest before God. Moses felt the burden of Israel and moaned before God in pain. Job was lonely and bewildered and gave God such a tongue-lashing. Elijah whined in his pain, and Jeremiah bitterly complained under his load. The psalmist (Ps. 73:2-3, 13-14) confessed that he had almost lost his faith, and Habakkuk is stunned by the fact that God was letting Judah away with murder. The writer of Ecclesiastes, with his "under the sun" vision (Eccles. 4:1; 5:8), wryly takes note of the corruption and oppression in the judiciary.

When we hotly protest or agonize in pain, we're in good company. The great men and women of God had their own questions while they writhed and wondered.

God never justifies our angry outbursts, but he has made it clear that he fully understands them. His dealing with Job, after Job has been insulting and openly offensive demonstrates this. His patience with Moses, his comforting of Elijah, his tolerance of Habakkuk and his listening to the psalmist tell us he doesn't throw a tantrum because we dare to voice a protest on behalf of the suffering. And this knowledge keeps people today from feeling they've committed unpardonable blasphemy or treachery when they blurt out their pain in the face of God.

The People With the Power To See It Through Don't Give Up on God

The same Moses who was displeased with God (Num. 11:10-15) ends his life singing God's praises (Deut. 31:30—33:29). And he does this despite the fact that God will not let him enter the promised land with Israel!

For all his insults, Job's commitment to God was deeper than that of his companions. Had Job simply dismissed God as cruel and unjust, he wouldn't have gone on protesting. No, Job's problem existed because he *knew* God was good and he couldn't work out how a good God could allow what was going on! His friends believed in a God who blessed those who kept their hands clean. (See Ps. 73:13.) Their blessed condition was proof that God was good. Take away their blessing and what? (See Ps. 1:9-11 and 2:9.) Job believed God was good and in essence tells God: "It isn't right for a good God to do this!" In the end, God commends Job who insisted on God's goodness despite the pain and rebukes the friends who viewed him as good because he always blessed the righteous (Job 42:7).

And Jeremiah, who bitterly compares God to a deceitful brook which is dry just when needed most (Jer. 15:18), is the one who writes Lamentations 3:22-24: "The steadfast love of the Lord never ceases, his mercies never come to an end; they are new every morning; great is thy faithfulness. 'The Lord is my portion,' says my soul, 'therefore I will hope in him' " (RSV). Was this written when everything had turned out all right? No, this was written while the smoke of forty-seven fortified cities was still going up, while Jewish dead were scattered for miles, while the smoking ruins of Jerusalem and the sanctuary were concrete realities and while fearful Jews were dragging Jeremiah off against his will to die in Egypt.

Look around you and see how many of your family, friends and acquaintances have looked suffering squarely in the eye and gone on to live radiant and productive lives. The last word on the lips of Jesus when he was going through his Golgotha hurricane was *"Father."*

The People With the Power To See It Through Don't View God as a "Heavenly Sweetheart"

Fosdick says so many preachers are "religious crooners" who sing nothing but romantic ballads about God. If we get too much of that stuff, God becomes froth and softness without an ounce of depth to him. It's clear from the Scriptures and from life that God is less interested in making our lives *easy* than he is in making them strong and clean and socially useful.

God's gentle but not soft. He won't always be tender, but he'll always be loving. He doesn't just want to be good to us, he wants us to be good and to be good one to another. It's obviously not his will to obliterate pain from human experience just by issuing an edict.

We teach little children the needed truths that God will aways "take care of" them, that he won't allow them to be harmed. But as quickly as we think it wise we balance this diet with other balancing truths lest we maim the child's growing understanding of God. God calls for, and we cooperate with him in the creating of, a mature faith. A faith which meets all that life confronts us with and which replaces a childish and oversimplified faith which, however useful as "kindergarten" material, is not suited to adults.

God doesn't "pick on" anybody, but he doesn't play favorites either. His *own* people get hurt in a world that knows a lot about pain. Christ never apologized for getting his followers into trouble. He often said they would suffer for his sake, but he never said: "I'm sorry about getting you in this trouble." The comfort he offered was this: "In the world you have tribulation; but be of good cheer, I have overcome the world" (Jn. 16:33; RSV).

This "soft view" of God can nearly wreck us when tragedy comes storming into our lives. Peter, whose views underwent a radical change between Matthew 16:22-23 and 1 Peter 4:12, urges believers not to think their suffering was a strange thing. Hardship is part of the price we pay for living in a world distorted by sin. In his spiritual infancy he thought suffering should play no part in God's scheme of things, but when he matured he understood that pain is part of the believer's inheritance. A God who works on those principles is no "heavenly sweetheart."

The People With the Power To See It Through Make Sure They Aren't Creating Their Own Pain

It isn't the first time that I've complained to God about my trouble and then discovered that the pain was of my own making. I suspect that more often than we care to admit, when we complain to God at his beating us, God's response could easily be: "I haven't laid a finger on you! This pain is your own creation!"

We can't insist on getting the wrong bus and expect to get to the right place. You can't play with fire and not expect to be burned. You can't indulge in gossip all the time and still expect to have close friends who trust you. You can't selfishly make endless demands on friends and not expect them to drift away from you and leave you lonely. You can't expect to be characterized by dishonor and still gain or retain the respect of your peers. You can't insist on being treacherous and still be free from ulcer-making fear that you'll be discovered.

Ivor Newell tells the story of Lokman the Wise. Lokman was an Arabian slave. His young master gave him good grain with which to sow his fields. Lokman prepared the ground, sowed the seed and it grew up into coarse and nearly worthless rye. The young master exploded, telling the servant he had given him good wheat grain and he had gotten this worthless rye. The servant replied that he had sowed the poor rye but had hoped good wheat would come up. The master was furious and demanded to know how Lokman could be so stupid. "Sir," said Lokman the Wise, "you are constantly sowing seeds of evil, selfishness and self-indulgence, and yet you talk as though virtue and character will grow. So I thought I might get a harvest of wheat from sowing poor rye!"

The People With the Power To See It Through Don't Lean Too Heavily on "Explanations"

Joseph Bayly got a letter from a woman. Here's what it said:

> On January 25th, 1973, in Memorial Hospital, John Riso, red-haired, laughing, tall, eighteen, tractor-driving, cow-scratching, flirtatious, shy, died after two and a half years of leukemia. After six weeks of a raging temperature, experimental drugs, bleeding, and an abscess in his rectum that became gangrenous, he died soft and gentle, finally, after six hours of violent death throes. His face so thin, his hair only a memory, a soft red fuzz, arms blue and green from shots and intravenous feeding, he looked like an old picture of a saint after his tortures were over. . . .
>
> Why would a kind God do what was done to John, or do such a thing to me? I'm poor, have only secondhand furniture and clothing. The things of value were my husband and sons. All our lives we've struggled to make ends meet. How can I live with the memory of the agony he suffered? . . . Part of the time he was in a coma, and he kept saying, "Mama, help me, Mama, help me." I couldn't and it's killing me. I whispered in his ear, "John, I love you so much." All of a sudden his arm came up stiffly and fell across my back, and very quietly he said, from some vast depth, "Me too."

Bayly, who lost three sons of his own, had no fully satisfying explanations to offer. The trouble with "explanations" is that they wear thin due to a lot of use. Besides, as Kushner and Bayly make clear, they're often worse than useless. Wild guesses are made about what God is trying to teach the grieving family, tentative suggestions and "maybes," comfortless remarks (even if they're true) about how suffering can make the family stronger, almost stupid remarks (under the circumstances) about God being glorified by the bravery of the sufferer—these are all commonplace.

It's all right, don't you understand, to look around for explanations and pointers if that's what your hurting heart needs and can use. But "explanations" mustn't be leaned on too heavily! Often the "explanation" is not only an insult to the sufferers (family and friends included), it is an insult to God!

A bad "explanation" only adds pain to pain!

It's right to attempt to justify the ways of God with men in regard to the existence of suffering and death in our world. Just the same, there's a very real sense in which God doesn't want to be "reconciled" to some of the evils in our world! Camus' point in the mouth of his agnostic doctor that people should "try to relieve human suffering before trying to point out its excellence" is well made.

The Christian needs to do more than "explain" it—he needs to do his bit to eradicate or alleviate it! Does Matthew 25 sound like this? "I was naked and you explained it. I was hungry and you made sound arguments. I was sick and you showed conclusively that a good God would still exist despite my sickness!" There are causes of disease, torment and death that Christians should be banding together in the name of God to ruthlessly hound right out of the world. Christians need to be known as those who promote better living here and now for the suffering masses as well as people who point the world to eternal realities.

Luke 7:17-23 has a hard saying but one that is full of help for us if we only make full use of it. John the Baptist has been imprisoned and sends two of his disciples to see what Jesus is going to do about it. He has them ask: "Are you he who is to come, or shall we look for another?"

Remembering that John has *known* Jesus is the Christ, we know we aren't dealing with serious doubts on John's part. No, it was the very report of his disciples of the miraculous power of Jesus Christ that leads John to make the inquiry (Lk. 7:18). What the man raised in the open spaces (Lk. 1:80) wanted to know was: "When are you going to get me out of here?" He must have hated his hole under the ground, and he had been faithful to the Christ. He had insisted on denying that he was the Messiah, insisted that his own disciples understand that he wasn't to be glorified but that Christ was to be glorified. He had withstood Herod's incestuous marriage to Herodias, his brother's wife. He had done all this, and now he lies in prison while Christ is liberating everyone else!

When the men come to Jesus, he makes them stand around while he heals multitudes (Lk. 7:20-21). Then he tells them to go tell John what they had seen and heard. See them going back to John. "What happened?" we can easily imagine John asking. "He made us stand around while he healed a host of people!" they would have said. "John, you have no idea how much power God has committed to that man!" Yes, yes, but did he say anything about getting John out of there? No, not a word! What did he say? He said John was to hear about all the people being liberated from disease and sin. But nothing about *John* being liberated? Nothing! And did he say anything else? Yes, John was to be told: "Blessed is the man who doesn't fall away on account of me" (Lk. 7:23).

Why did Jesus make those men witness this incredible power before sending them back to John? And what did he mean by "blessed is he who doesn't find me someone to stumble over"? He was telling John: "John, I'm not getting you out of prison. Not because I *can't*, but because I don't choose to! But trust me, just the same!"

There are few things that try our faith more, somebody said, than God doing all kinds of lovely things for others while refusing to do them for us. There aren't many tests of trust as severe as God answering the prayers of others and taking away their burden while saying *no* to ours and leaving the load heavy on us.

And John gets no explanation! Not so much as "but I want you to know I have good reasons for this!" There is implicit in the words of Christ that he understands John could take offense at all this, but he takes that risk and asks John to trust him without explanation. *And John does!*

Henri Nouwen thoughtfully remarks that it might be the minister's chief function to deliver people from *meaningless* suffering.

If the minister succeeds in doing that for anyone, it won't be by giving a tailor-made explanation for every affliction in life. That isn't possible! But if we can see the God who revealed himself in Jesus Christ, the God who showed himself most clearly *in* (not just through) the suffering on the cross, we'll know that sense can be made of it all.

The two thieves on the crosses experienced the same torments. They both yelled derision at the Christ; they both insisted that if he had power all three of them would be delivered from pain. Then one of them was caught by the Christ; his heart was changed by the silent Sufferer, and his suffering became a secondary issue! The "explanation" which would deliver us from a savage bitterness at what looks like meaningless suffering would be a long, understanding look at the heart of the God who spoke to us out of the darkness of his own awful pain. Would a God such as this, who is pained by our pain, who so loves us that he will not let us suffer alone, allow it, if for some reason it did not have to be?

There, in the final analysis, is the "explanation" which satisfies the hearts of those who have the power to see it through. *A God like Jesus Christ would never be loveless!*

The People With the Power To See It Through Ask Themselves, "Why Not Me?" Rather Than, "Why Me?"

God help us, sometimes we think it's God's supreme business to keep us from getting hurt. I don't mean to be rude in saying that! And if you're in severe pain at this time, please don't take it as a callous insult. I'm speaking about an attitude which must change if we are to find any joy in a world of suffering.

Countless thousands have suffered before us that they might do us some great service. People have died that we might have the Bible available to us. Medical researchers have burned their lives away in search of cures for diseases which used to sweep away millions who suffered terribly before they died. Scientists and statesmen, teachers and humanitarians have shortened their lives and suffered much just to bless us. Mothers and fathers have done without that we might have. They've chosen less that we might have more. And Christ suffered for us!

And if the time should come that we are to suffer greatly, should we think it not our turn? If there are people who must be taught to live radiantly and hopefully in spite of suffering, would it be unfair of God if he should ask us to do that for them? Or must all the suffering be endured by others? Are we and ours alone to be exempted? Kipling speaks of people like that, people who gave up what they could have claimed, that others might be blessed.

People who set aside their Today,
All the joys of their Today,
And with the toil of their Today,
Bought for us Tomorrow.

But it's just at this point that people stumble. If they *knew* their suffering or the suffering of those they love had *purpose*, they could bear it more easily. If they thought it had *significant* purpose, that it was going to bring something about that was worth the price paid, they would be able to bear it. Since they can't see any point or meaning to it all they despair. Viktor Frankl said: "Despair is meaningless suffering." There's a lot of truth in that!

When reporters asked Mrs. Einstein if she understood Einstein's theory of relativity, she thought for a moment and then said: "No, but you can trust Albert!" We may not always understand God's way, but Christ comes saying to us: "You can trust my Father!"

If God came to each of us every morning and briefed us on what was going to happen that day, I suspect that would make it easier for us to take. If he told us we were going to suffer and explained how that could be fitted into his overall plan, we'd feel better about our suffering. *But he doesn't and he won't!* (See later in the chapter on *keeping the cross at the center*.)

And it might well be, that even if God came to us to tell us how our pain could be used redemptively, we would still protest: Why me? It is *this* kind of attitude we need to guard against. We speak of how we admire those who suffer radiantly and redemptively for others. We thrill and glow at the memory of those who gave everything and at those who bear their pain bravely. *What should we do when it is our turn to act nobly?*

The People With the Power To See It Through Remember That Judgment Day Is Coming

Genesis 18:25 assures us that the Judge of all the earth will do what's right. (See Rom. 3:4-6.) To long for justice isn't vindictiveness! It isn't evil to want evil dealt with! *God is going to right all wrongs!* It's plain to see that almost all the suffering in the world could be eliminated if Man would stop brutalizing Man and, under God, work for the blessing of his neighbor. The bulk of suffering in the world could be eased and/or eradicated if Man wasn't sinful!

Just to know that someone is going to answer for the pain poured out on the heads of the defenseless is some comfort! The butchering of over two million Cambodians by Pol Pot and his Khmer Rouge is going to be dealt with! The slaughter of multiplied millions by Ghengis Khan, Stalin, Papa Doc, Ashurbanipal, Hitler, the Shah of Iran and their lackeys is all going to be dealt with. The murder and torture of unnamed and countless thousands by western military forces, the exploitation and impoverishing of the politically naive nations by western governments and huge companies, all this will be answered for! The drug lords of the world will be called to account for the countless thousands they have tormented and ruined.

Several weeks ago, the news report told us a man and his live-in lover were being tried in connection with the death of one of his children (he had two little boys). The partly decomposed body of the younger child was discovered by police who had been called in by social workers. The other child was absolutely skin and bone. The only food in the house was dog food! Plenty of it! The dog was in perfect health! The two people were unemployed, they had $320 per week coming in and they spent almost all of it at a pub just across the street. Both of them were *very* overweight! They were tried for manslaughter. This kind of thing has become absolutely epidemic in the U.K.

All of this positive inflicting of torture, this sophisticated exploitation of the masses and the selfish refusal of nations to band together to beat disease and crime—it will all be answered for!

But what of those already tortured to death? What of those who have already been emotionally butchered beyond recall? What of those who have been robbed from the cradle to the grave? *Think noble things of God! All wrongs will be righted!* The Judge of all the earth will do what is right! Remember the words of Mrs. Einstein about Albert (see above), and trust God to work it all out!

The People With the Power To See It Through Are Comforted by Helping Others

Have you ever read George Eliot's *Silas Marner*? Recently? If not, do it or do it again. The hero, Silas Marner, was a linen weaver who bothered little with people. His religion left him with more fear than hope for the future in another world. Silas had two friends, a girl called Sarah, whom he was planning to marry, and William Dane, whom he trusted implicitly. He is unjustly accused of robbing a dead man. His friend William (who really stole the money) speaks against Marner, and the church finds him guilty. Marner, who was convinced that God would see him through this crisis, accuses Dane of stealing the money and of weaving a plot to blame the weaver. His faith snaps and he cries: "*You* stole the money . . . But you may prosper, for all that: there is no just God that governs the earth righteously, but a God of lies, that bears witness against the innocent."

Sarah breaks the engagement and marries William Dane. Silas Marner leaves town and comes to Raveloe where he works himself into the ground. Always at the loom, eyesight deteriorating, bothering with no one, a virtual recluse, nursing his bitterness and hoarding his coins. He is almost a dead man! When a charitable act toward a sick woman leads the village to think of him as being in league with some mysterious powers, his isolation is complete!

He is robbed of all his money which by now is the only source of comfort to him in all the world. He plunges into hell from which he is redeemed by the arrival of a baby girl. The mother dies not far from Silas' door, and the child wanders into the light and heat of the fireside. The rest of the book is a marvelous portrayal of Marner's resurrection and salvation by his taking upon himself the burdens of someone else!

Joe Bayly, a marvelous sufferer, urges all those who wrestle in pain, to seek out someone needy and minister to their needs and find consolation there. Does he say it's easy? No! Vincent de Paul, one of the world's most experienced students of suffering, would continually remind people that it was the greatest sufferers who found the greatest comfort in ministering to the needs of others.

John Bright was one of England's bright young statesmen of the nineteenth century. His young wife died, and Bright lamented: "I was in the depths of grief—I may almost say despair, for the light and the sunshine of my house had been extinguished . . . Mr. Cobden called on me. . . ." Richard Cobden, who founded the Anti-Corn Law League in the "hungry forties," having offered his sincere condolences sat in silence for a considerable time. Finally he arose and gently said to Bright: "There are thousands and thousands of homes in England at this moment where wives and mothers and children are dying of hunger. Now, when the first paroxysm of your grief is passed, I would advise you to come with me, and we will never rest until the Corn Laws are repealed." Those who have the power to see it through have found consolation in taking upon them the burdens of others. *Is this part of the reason God has called us to "bear one another's burdens"?*

The People With the Power To See It Through Keep the Cross of Christ Central In Their Thinking

The One on the cross didn't cry: "How can there be a God when this is going on?" He groaned his pain, he cried his loneliness, he voiced his appeals, but it never entered his mind to doubt the existence of God! Nor did it enter his mind to thrust God aside as unworthy of worship or service! His pained outburst still says, "*My* God, *my* God, why hast thou . . . ?"

Christ has shown us that it's all right to cry when we hurt! It's all right to express the inner storm through the lips! Christ tells us we don't have to pretend we're not hurt!

And because Jesus Christ is the Representative Man, he voiced for all of us the bitterness of suffering and the agony of bewilderment. In Jesus, *mankind* expresses its painful confusion and the hurt that lies behind and under the hurt.

And in Jesus Christ (who is God *with* us), God has joined us in our pain. He's no spectator. It is *God* who is in Christ reconciling the world to himself by the cross! It is *God* who becomes the Representative Man, enduring suffering at its most brutal and senseless level and investing it with dignity and meaning. Yes! Investing it with dignity and meaning! Making it redemptive. In a world without Sin that would not be necessary, but this isn't a world without Sin!

In Jesus Christ, God comes speaking to us. He teaches us that we shouldn't look away from suffering to find him because the greatest revelation of God takes place *in* suffering. He challenges us to look long at the cross and draw the conclusion that God isn't absent there, isn't nonexistent there, but is never more fully revealed than there! But how can we see him there when such suffering compels us to speak of "forsakenness"? We speak of "forsakenness" because God wouldn't intervene to stop this awful brutalizing of Man by men (hence the "abandonment"). But God wouldn't let mankind bear this pain alone, so he joined us in the Man who represents us all!

In Jesus Christ we learn that the presence of pain doesn't mean the absence of God! In him we learn that God can use pain redemptively! In the cross God suffers *for* us and *with* us and *from* us (Moltmann). In the cross we learn God isn't a "heavenly sweetheart" and has no intention of always intervening to bring suffering to a halt. Wasn't it Christ himself who spurned Peter's military solution? Wasn't it Christ who *insisted*, for all his human reaction to it, on drinking the cup the Father had for him? Wasn't it Christ himself who rebuked the two disciples on the road to Emmaus for taking the *glory* passages and dismissing the *suffering* ones (Lk. 24:25-26)? And wasn't it the Master himself who rasped at Peter to get out of his way with his devilish talk of "no suffering" (Mt. 16:21-24)? *The people with the power to see it through keep these things in mind.*

The People With the Power To See It Through Know That Suffering Can Be Bravely Borne

The cross is more than a brave man bearing suffering, but it *is* that! At the heart of the Christian's faith is a Man who was bloodied but ultimately unbowed. And millions throughout the centuries saw that bravery and were moved to bravery by it.

McGrath reminds us that it is a modern view that suffering must drive us to atheism. The "problem of suffering" has been seen for as long as there have been thinking men and women. The Bible is full of this wrestling. Countless generations of people knew there was a "problem" in all this, but they never dreamed of dumping God! But healthy and well-situated philosophizers have urged the real sufferers to take a God-rejecting stance. For all their talk, they fail to succeed. The masses never give up on God, at least not over the suffering problem.

The rank and file of men and women are too courageous. They make less of their (very real) sufferings than the "talkers" who know nothing of pain! You can see it all around you. Read *The City of Joy* by Dominic Lapierre and be thrilled at the bravery of sufferers. *Real* sufferers. Read of the creative responses of people like Stephan Kovalski, Louis Pasteur, Beethoven, Robert L. Stevenson, May Lempke, Terry Fox and a thousand other well known people. Look at the smiles of thousands of parents of children with Down's syndrome or spina bifida. Listen for the stories of bravery and radiance coming out of prison camps, hospitals, ghetto slums and prisons.

Countless sufferers, *real* sufferers have made it clear to us that *suffering isn't Lord*! They will *not* be victims! They don't have the time for endless self-pity; they have too much they can and feel they want to do! Not all sufferers take this approach (and I've no criticisms to offer here for those who don't), but there are enough of them in every street, of every village, town, city and metropolis in every country of the world to make it clear that they're bigger than their suffering!

I loved the *Rocky* movies. Every one of them! They all had the same plot: a decent man fighting for personal dignity against great odds! In *Rocky III*, a 230-pound human wrecking-machine called Clubber Lang had given Rocky a bad beating. But he did more than that. He had humiliated him. The fight at the close of the movie shows an unsure Rocky begin to really come on strong. In order to regain what he had lost (personal dignity), he has to soak up punishment. All the punishment this powerful clod could dish out. Each punch seems like it would rip Rocky's head off, but he came back for more. Lang is handing it out, and it's making no dent in the man he wants to shame and humiliate. He punches even harder, but his victim is free. "Come on," says the hero, "hit me again!" His former tormentor does just that, and Rocky yells at him: "It ain't so bad! Ain't so bad!" Lang redoubles his efforts, but Rocky taunts him: "Ain't so bad. You ain't so bad!" And the movie concludes with the hero finding the power to see it through. I loved it! Every now and then when Ethel is having one of her *especially* bad days, we look at each other, smile and say: "Ain't so bad! It ain't so bad!"

What doesn't destroy us, said the atheist Nietzsche, makes us strong! Our trials, said Paul, bring approvedness (Rom. 5). Our trials, said Peter, strengthen and purify our faith (1 Pet. 1). The trials, said James, work endurance in us (Jas. 1). If you have dreams that matter to you, principles that sustain you, suffering can be bravely borne. I want to *know* Christ, said Paul, and so I choose suffering (Phil. 3).

The movie *Jeremiah Johnson* is the story of a city man who wants to become a "mountain man." His mountain career is full of pain, tears, loneliness and grief. He spends years fighting for survival in the cold and many months in fighting to survive against a tribe of Indians who send assassins, one by one, to take his life. Near the close of the movie, an old mountain man who had taught him some things, comes by Johnson's fire and gets around to asking the now hardy mountain man: "Well, pilgrim, was it worth all the trouble?" Johnson thought for a second or two and then asked: "What trouble?" I loved it!

I smile now and then when I read some pathetic philosophizer who tells us that suffering proves God doesn't care and turn to read about or listen to someone who has *deliberately chosen* awful suffering in the name of God and for the welfare of the people. People like some Moravian missionaries who years ago went to a leper valley in Tangier to share Christ with the hopeless there. The authorities told them if they went in they wouldn't be allowed out again. They spent the day in prayer, kissed their families goodbye, went in and were never seen again. I throw such philosophizing books aside when I read of Catholic priests who were waiting on board a ship, seeking permission from the Chinese to enter and share their faith. Entry was being refused to foreign religious teachers. One slipped off the ship one night and returned a few days later to excitedly tell his colleagues that he had found a way in. They had themselves sold into slavery and never saw each other again.

I'm just wanting to make the point that suffering can be chosen and/or bravely used if it comes unbidden. I'm not saying that this is the rule because I know that millions wither under suffering, that they are warped and never recover. I'm just saying, we don't *have* to be victims! Viktor Frankl, whose awful sufferings give him a clear right to speak, insists that it isn't what happens to us that counts, but what we do with what happens to us.

Don Williams told of a little boy in Midland, Texas, who fell at school and cut his head. Later he collided with another boy and got a couple of loose teeth and facial swelling. And later still he fell and broke his arm. The principal, Mr. Chapman, decided to take him home before something else happened. As he was driving him home, the man noticed the boy was grasping something in his hand. He asked him what it was, and the boy showed him a shiny new quarter. "Where did you get it?" asked the principal. "I found it in the playground!" the lad responded. Then silence. The boy broke it with: "You know, sir, I've never found a quarter before. This is my lucky day!" Don't you love that story! That's the stuff heroes are made of. Cut head, loose teeth, swollen mouth, broken arm and "this is my lucky day!"

I don't believe that suffering in and of itself is good! And I believe that God would have us alleviate or eliminate such needless pain as we can. Camus' word keeps ringing in my ears. The man is right on that point. Just the same, we have put suffering on one end of the spectrum and glory or joy on the other—Paul put them both together in Romans 8:17!

Do you remember how the rabbit gave the fox such a hard time? When the fox finally *did* get hold of the rabbit he didn't only want to eat him, he wanted to give him pain. . . . P-A-I-N! "I think," he said with mean eyes glittering, "I think I'll *skin* you!" The rabbit gulped and stuttered: "Sure, you do that. Skin me, but whatever you do, don't throw me in that briar patch!" The fox's glittering eyes took in at a glance the inch-long, needle-sharp barbs. . . . hmmmm.

With dripping malice he rattled: "I think I'll boil you in oil!" "Yes, sure!" whined the rabbit. "Boil me in oil (gulp). Do anything. But there's one thing I'm begging you, please don't do! Don't throw me in that awful briar patch!" The menacing eyes of the fox took a long look at the flesh-tearing, agony-bringing, soul-tormenting thorns, and he became convinced that the worst thing in the world that could happen to that rabbit was for it to be thrown into the briar patch. High in the air he flung him. Down into the jungle of ripping, gouging daggers he fell. Then silence. Then rabbit laughter and a taunting song: "I was born and bred in the old briar patch, the old briar patch, the old briar patch."

The people of God faced that kind of malice from the day they were born. A brutal and sadistic world thought that the worst thing that could happen to the church of God was to persecute it, give it pain, shed its blood. But like Israel of old, the more it was oppressed the more it grew, and fair-minded, courageous people streamed into its ranks, drawn by the good news it proclaimed and seized by the power of the living Christ who indwelt them by his Spirit.

Suffering and pain had been used against their Master. Did the silly world think it would work against his disciples when it had so miserably failed against him? They were born in trouble; their birth came out of suffering; their destiny was to get to know their Lord by becoming partakers of his sufferings so that they could even in this life experience the power which raised him from the dead! Pain won't beat us; suffering won't harm us. Christ always knew that the cross wouldn't do him any harm! And it won't do his Body any harm either—it's end is glory!

But you're afraid of suffering? Yes, and why not? God doesn't require that we be Stoics! Jesus was no Stoic as we can see from the garden of Gethsemane record. There's a difference between a masochist and a brave person. Brave people go ahead and pursue what's right even when they're frightened or weeping.

Henri de Turenne, the brave French military leader during the Thirty Years' War, was a man of deep piety and integrity. Just before going into battle he was shaving and his hand trembled violently. He looked at his body and thundered: "You're trembling, vile carcass? You would tremble more if you knew where I am going to take you this day!" He went and behaved honorably. They later made him marshall general in 1660. *This* is the kind of response people have shown themselves capable of when wrestling with their fears.

The People With the Power To See It Through Let the Resurrection Have the Last Word

The One who was brutally murdered on the cross is the Representative of *mankind*. In him we see all the faces of all the exploited and oppressed. Focused in him we see all the humans of all the ages dying as a result of Sin. He represents all the voiceless, the defenseless, the forgotten, the weary, the bewildered—the sinful and the innocent! In his own experience, suffering and death speak most clearly. In his loving healings, he takes to his heart the disease and pain of the sick (Mt. 8:16-17), but he does it on the cross in the fullest possible way.

And the resurrection is the message God gives us that suffering and death don't have the final word; that the last word is with LIFE!

The world sees the suffering in the Gulag prison system and in the death camps of Auschwitz and Buchenwald as incapable of yielding any sense under any scheme, as unrelievable emptiness. *But Golgotha is Auschwitz!* Golgotha is the Russian labor camps! God has shown himself there in those very situations. Golgotha, Auschwitz and Siberia have all one thing in common—they are the work of sinful man! They are the work of sinful man against himself!

Alone and without the resurrection, Golgotha is unrelieved and unrelievable gloom (1 Cor. 15:14, 17-18). But in light of the resurrection we learn to see God *in* the Auschwitz called Golgotha and in the Golgotha called Auschwitz. The resurrection is the proof that God was there! That *God* was enduring the pain! That *God* was identified with and *was* the suffering one there! "In doing it to the least of these my brothers, you did it to me!" "Saul, Saul, why are you persecuting me?" In light of the resurrection, he who groaned in his feelings of forsakenness, was Mankind groaning in its sense of abandonment. In light of the resurrection it was both God and Man *together* who experienced the vast depths of pain.

And the resurrection says evil loses! The resurrection says suffering and death lose! The resurrection says, in the words of a black evangelist, *Friday's over, Sunday's come!* Suffering's bad, but it's day is Friday. Death is bad, but it's beaten, because Sunday has come! Bad Friday became Good Friday because Sunday rolled around.

Every blade of grass coming out of the ground after a bitter winter is God's reminder that LIFE wins! Every blossom that heralds the coming of fruit after the tree has gone through the howling cold of a winter season shouts at us that death loses!

I had my driveway covered. The workers came and took away some earth and rolled the area flat. Then they came with three million tons of gravel and spread it over the whole area and rolled it flat! They then poured forty million tons of hot, sticky, tarry gravel over that and rolled it down flat. Finally they brought one hundred and thirty two million tons more of that material, spread it and rolled it down—flat!

"No more weeds in that driveway!" I smugly mused. A couple of months later I parked my car and stubbed my toe on something on the driveway surface. A little molehill. Created by a feeble little stem which had been buried way down there in the dark. I looked around, and there they were, about a dozen of them all pushing their way up through all that weight and pressure to get through to the light! God was saying to me: "Just wanted to remind you!"

O Thou, most righteous Father, who hast suffered so much in the suffering of thy Son, teach us that we are not alone.

O thou, most blessed Savior, who wast perfected in suffering that you might ransom our poor souls, inspire us to live like you.

O thou, most needed Spirit of God, who has been grieved and caused to suffer through our suffering and evil, be our helper against the pleadings of our soft flesh which would have us refuse our cross.

O thou Holy Trinity, forgive us our cowardly whimpering, silence our moaning with strong love, point us to others who suffer without comfort and use us as thy channels of blessing. And may we, in easing their pain, healing their wounds, not only teach them of thy loving heart, find our own hurts strangely healed. Amen.

3

Redemptive Relationships

I should like to add a beatitude: Blessed is the man who gives us back our self-respect.

MARK RUTHERFORD

Jean Valjean, my brother, you no longer belong to what is evil but to what is good. I have bought your soul to save it from black thoughts and the spirit of perdition, and I give it to God.

VICTOR HUGO
in *Les Misérables*

And Saul's son Jonathan went to David at Horesh and helped him find strength in God.

1 SAMUEL 23:16

What a great man accomplishes for the world is this: he does something that was never done before but which once it is done, becomes a standard for the rest of us, below which we can no longer be content.

WORDSWORTH

Think instead of your mother's hand patting you on the head, just heavily enough to tell you that your most important person thinks you are a good child, good enough for her to love you. . . . One whopping hand-clap is like a Lourdes for a crippled ego. Then there is the soft stroke, the intimate brush . . . a wish for you to know that you are able to fill another's life with joy.

LEWIS SMEDES

The People With
The Power To See It Through
Experience . . .

Redemptive Relationships

God saves people through people! And the Devil crushes people through people! For good or ill, people influence our lives. Those who enjoy the power to see it through have relationships which inspire them, relationships, which by the grace of God, contribute to God's ongoing redemptive work in their lives.

Most often, I suppose, we find redeeming relationships within the family. Timothy found this to be true. In 2 Timothy 1:5 we learn that Timothy found his mother and grandmother to be God's instruments of his salvation. From infancy he was taught the Scriptures (2 Tim. 3:14-15), and there's little doubt who would have done that.

Grandmothers have so often been God's unsung heroes. They have so often been the unsung heroes of children. When they asked a little boy what a grandmother was, he said something like: "Grandmothers are ladies who have no children of their own so they love everybody else's. They're fat, but not too fat to tie your shoes. They usually wear glasses and sometimes they can take their teeth out. They can answer all the questions like, why dogs hate cats and if God's married. When they take you for walks they don't keep telling you to hurry up if you want to stop and look at something. And when they read you a story they never skip any lines even if they've read it a lot of times before. Everybody should try to have a grandmother, especially if they don't have a TV, because grandmothers are the only grown-ups who always have time for you." (*Be somebody special to somebody!*)

Lewis Smedes has some lovely things to say about saving relationships within the family circle. He reminds us of our childhood when either father or mother patted us on the head just hard enough to tell us that the most important person in our lives thought we were good children. And what about the backslapping we get from our friends? Isn't that great? The pain we endure is the price we pay for the assurance that we are one of the gang! And sometimes, if you're lucky, says Smedes, you get one whopping good round of applause which is like a Lourdes to a crippled ego! Down inside all of us, down where the little boy or girl survives in us, we need somebody's pat on the head, somebody's slap on the back, somebody's warm applause just to give us the power to see it through. (*What am I going to do about what I'm writing here?*)

And doesn't human love just amaze you at times? Haven't we all been loved by someone long after we've lost any "right" to be loved?! Have you never advised a wife who's been beaten senseless week after week by a drunken husband, "Leave him or have him put out of the house"? She knows you care, but she smiles and says something about loving him no matter what he is.

The missionary doctor to Labrador, Wilfred Grenfell, told of a night when a woman was brought into the hospital, dying of terrible burns. The facts were that her husband had come home drunk and thrown the kerosene lamp over her. The police and the husband were there by her bed while the magistrate quietly asked her to tell what happened. The husband, miserable and frightened, listened intently. "I can see to this day," said Grenfell, "the magistrate stooping over the bed warning her she had but a few minutes to live. . . . He kept imploring her to tell the truth, as he took her dying statement. At last her eyes were raised to the face of the man, the father of her children, the man who had sworn so shortly before to love and protect her 'until death do us part.' Here he was now, her murderer. The silence at her bedside, as we waited for her reply, could be felt. As her eyes fell upon the familiar features, I can only suppose she saw him as once he had been, before drink claimed him as another victim. For a new light came into them as she passed out with a lie on her lips to save him. 'My God! It was an accident!' was the last thing she said."

Yes, yes, make whatever comments you wish to make on this event, but don't miss the tremendous power in it. I don't know what happened to the man after this; I only know of the inspiring example that woman is of the longing to save someone who had no right to look for mercy!

But the spirit of this occasion isn't new. Didn't Paul himself blurt out something like: "If it could save my kinsmen, I could see myself cut off from Christ!" (Be sure to see the text—Rom. 9:3.) What a daring thing to say! What a puzzling thing to say! And yet, what a loving thing to say. The redemptive spirit is in this. The spending of oneself for someone else. The doing of costly things on behalf of others. *Is this not the message of the cross?*

And Paul's inner turmoil helps explain the incident involving an old British chieftain of centuries ago. He was stepping down into the baptistry to be baptized into the Christ when he posed his question. He said to the preacher: "And what has happened to all my forefathers who died unbaptized?" The minister told him they were burning in hell. For a long time the old chieftain stood there in the water, silent. Then he turned and walked back up the steps as he wrapped his wolfskin robe around him. Gently he said: "I believe I'll take my chances with them!" Qualify the man's response as you see you must, but don't deny the power of it. Don't resist the inspiration that flows from such loyalty. *It's that kind of loyalty which drives people to noble and redemptive living.*

We saw it in Jonathan, son of Saul, didn't we?! In 1 Samuel 23:15-18, when David was hounded and broken-spirited, Jonathan came and "helped him find strength in God." Jonathan, the king's son, risked his father's fury in remaining loyal and inspirational to David. Even knowing that David would inherit the kingdom rather than himself, Jonathan still kept David from going under.

And Barnabas was a good friend. His relationships with people were always redemptive. Early in Acts we find him lovingly redeeming the poor from need. Later we find him redeeming the newly converted Paul from isolation and bringing him into the warm fellowship of the saints. And later still we find him putting his arm around Mark's shoulder when Paul refused to have the young man around him on a proposed missionary journey. "He isn't going with us," we can hear Paul say. "He isn't dependable!" We can easily imagine Barnabas making excuses for the lad and asking for another chance for him. "Too many things are at stake," Paul might have exclaimed. "He already got his chance and whimpered off home when things got tough." What we're certain of is this, Barnabas vigorously opposed one of the most determined men in history for the sake of "the quitter." And as the biblical story of it all concludes, Barnabas, by God's grace, has so transformed the boy that Paul confesses his need of him during a very trying time indeed. (See Acts 15:36-39 and 2 Tim. 4:11.)

William Hale White (better known as "Mark Rutherford") said: "I should like to add a beatitude: Blessed is the man who gives us back our self-respect." Barnabas did that for Mark, and Abraham Lincoln did that for Ross McIntyre. McIntyre had shown cowardice in the face of battle and was to be executed. Lincoln gave the man a full pardon in a letter which is kept in Washington to this day. The letter offered a full pardon to the deserter saying that he had promised to honorably fulfill all that was asked of him from that time forward. He was killed in the very last battle of the war at the point where the fighting had been hottest. The letter was found on the man. Lincoln had given him back his self-respect. Brief though his contact with Lincoln was, it was redemptive!

You come across this in really great literature, don't you?! Do you remember Jean Valjean, the hero of Hugo's classic, *Les Misérables*? He had been unjustly treated, imprisoned, and over the years he had become a hardened criminal, an embittered man. After his release he found himself spending the night in the house of an old bishop who (even though he knows Valjean's condition) treats him with extraordinary kindness. In the middle of the night Valjean silently leaves the house with the household silver, but he is picked up by the police who bring him back to the bishop's house.

As they enter with Valjean the old bishop steps quickly forward and says: "So here you are! I'm delighted to see you. Had you forgotten that I gave you the candlesticks as well? They're silver like the rest, and worth a good two hundred francs. Did you forget to take them?" After dismissing the astonished police but before he lets Valjean go, the old bishop tells the speechless one: "Jean Valjean, my brother, you no longer belong to what is evil but to what is good. I have bought your soul to save it from black thoughts and the spirit of perdition, and I give it to God." *Doesn't that make you want to smile?!* The rest of the book is the story of a redeemed man living like a redeemed man!

And who stirs the hearts of such authors to write such lovely things? Why, who else but Jesus Christ himself! He whose example from beginning to end redeemed men and gave them back their self-respect! In John 21 when he forced Peter to confess three times what he had denied three times, Christ was redeeming Peter. Knowing *everything* (21:17b), he still commissions Peter, and the rest of the story we know from the book of Acts and other places. Everyone who has had a heart for lovely things and has learned of Jesus Christ has been inspired to do wonderful things!

Years ago Quiller Couch told us that in his young days everyone writing in Britain was writing with one eye on an island in the South Pacific where Robert Louis Stevenson was living out the rest of his life, troubled as always with illness. They wrote, he told us, with the hope that Stevenson would hear of their work and not think it too unworthy. Isn't that wonderful?! And isn't it true that down through the centuries men and women have been living their lives with one eye on Nazareth! Hoping that Jesus Christ, when he glimpsed their lives, would not think them too trivial or unworthy!

Sir Thomas Foxwell Burton knew what it was like to have a redemptive relationship. In his youthful years, though everyone knew he had the makings of real manhood in him, he had no fire or purpose to give them shape. That's when he met up with the Earlham family.

Here's what he wrote many years later of his ties with that family:

> I know no blessing of a temporal nature for which I ought to render so many thanks as my connection with the Earlham family; it has given color to my whole life. They were eager for improvement; I caught the infection. At the college of Dublin, at a distance from all my friends and all control, their influence and the desire to please them kept me hard at my books and sweetened the toil they gave. The distinctions I gained at college were exclusively the result of the animating passion in my mind to carry back to them the prizes which they prompted and enabled me to win.

Yes! Haven't you experienced that? Of course you have! We've all "showed off" in that innocent sense when we tried very hard to please someone or to make them smile. There have been people in our lives for love of whom we would have fought a nine-headed, hundred-armed giant. They took us (at least for a while) out of our self-pity or aimlessness and gave us something better to do and *want* to do!

The world, whether it believes it or not, has a crying need for good models! Wasn't it Schweitzer who said: "Example isn't the best way to teach—it is the only way!"? Exaggeration? Of course! But by how much? The power of a model is seen in the statistics on alcoholism and child abuse. It's commonplace for alcoholics or child abusers to have been raised in a home environment like that where parents or some influential family member modeled this. (Other homes offered so little warm influence that the child got it all outside the home, from peers.)

Years ago, said Exum, before TV, when radio was

king, an old shepherd away out in the "boondocks" wrote to a radio station asking them if they could do him a favor. He wanted to take up playing the violin and needed someone to strike an "A" for him. The station master arranged it and on a given day, after chatting to the old man for a while, a local orchestra leader struck an "A" and held it for thirty seconds. I love that story. All that trouble just so some unknown old man could make music. He knew what an "A" was—he needed it modeled for him! And we all know so much more than we can live up to. We've had plenty of "talkers." But there is a real need for more than "talkers." (That's one of the reasons God sent Jesus Christ to us as a model—1 Pet. 2:21.)

Not only do we all need heroes, we all have them (yes, I know what Jane Fonda said, but she has them like the rest of us).

But there are dangers in endlessly parading heroes. *First*, a steady diet of heroes can lead us to despise the ordinary. *Second*, a steady diet of heroes can lead us to despise ourselves. *Third*, a steady diet of heroes can lead us to despise the work of God in us and to be ungrateful for the progress we've made. *Fourth*, a steady diet of heroes can lead us to judge people in a cruel way, without taking into account the factors which made one a "hero" and another "ordinary."

But if we keep all that in mind, it's still true that heroes help us to believe in ourselves. They help us to believe that we can, by God's grace, respond honorably to life's challenges and problems. They help us to believe that we who are pathetic prisoners (at times) of an alien power can, by God's goodness, do brave things, pure things, loving things as well as *dream* lovely dreams.

Wordsworth put it like this: *"What a great man accomplishes for the world is this: he does something that was never done before but which once it is done, becomes a standard for the rest of us, below which we can no longer be content."*

This "model" activity is in the mind of Peter when he speaks of Christ as our example (1 Pet. 2:21). And listen to Christ in John 17:19: "For them I sanctify myself, that they too may be truly sanctified." Paul calls fellow-disciples to follow his example where it honored the Christ (1 Cor. 11:1; 1 Thess. 2:1-12).

In life and in literature we find wondrous models to keep before us. Read of these people and be shaken out of complacency. People like May Lempke, Kagawa, Stephan Kovalski, Helen Keller and Annie Sullivan, Damien, Livingstone and Corrie Ten Boom. Read the great literature and be lifted by Sydney Carton in *A Tale of Two Cities*, or Esmeralda in *Hunchback of Notre Dame*, or Lorna in Hawthorne's *Lorna Doone* and on and on.

We're so accustomed to the *less* that we forget there is *more*. We're so surrounded by the *complacent* that we fail to dream after the *consecrated*. We live with the *lackluster* and rarely aspire to the *splendid*. As Tozer said, we are so used to unholiness we've come to look for no more than "fairly decent." Harry E. Fosdick had provocative things to say about all this.

He said people divided into three classes, the lawless, the law-abiding and those who obey self-imposed law. Listen to this:

> Perilous to society as lawless folk are, the second class is our greater danger. There are many more of them; every one of us is tempted to belong with them—the barely good, who get by on the conduct that is required.

We *expect* mothers to take care of their children, and when they do, we're pleased but not amazed. Such people don't *inspire* us in the way May Lempke does! What possessed a fifty-two-year-old, 4½-foot-tall, ninety-pound woman to take on an infant of six months who was blind, mentally retarded and had cerebral palsy?

What drove her to devote herself to him until he could give joy and inspiration to millions? She lovingly coaxed this out of a child others insisted should be institutionalized and a child many today insist should have been "put down" in infancy. *And it cost her a great deal, she and her husband, Joe!*

When they looked for the possessions of *W. C. Burns,* they found he had nothing but a Chinese Bible, an English Bible, the clothes he wore and a writing case. He died far from his Scottish home preaching to the Chinese attendants around his bed in a remote spot he had chosen to visit because of its destitution. *Toyohiko Kagawa* lived fifteen years in a 6'x6' hut to bring Christ to the exploited. For over four years he slept holding the hand of a murderer who couldn't sleep without someone holding his hand. Slum bullies would break his nose, knock his teeth out and make him take to his heels when he saw them coming. They laughed a lot about it, but he was always back the next day preaching to little groups wherever he could find them. On a visit to Harvard a couple of listening students weren't too impressed. One said to the other: "He didn't really have a lot to say, did he?!" A lady behind them leaned over and said: "When you're hanging on a cross you don't need to say much!"

Then there was *John Williams* who spent twenty-three restless years speaking about Christ in the South Seas islands before finally being murdered and eaten by natives in Erromanga. Matthewman speaks again and again of his "longing" to take the gospel to those who hadn't heard. Within eighteen years, so dedicated was he to spreading the word that "no island of importance within two thousand miles of Tahiti had been left unvisited." And on it goes!

People like these, by God's grace, redeem our faith in human potential under God. They "give us back our self-respect." They help us to want more than simply to be law-abiding. What they do in their own life is marvelous, but it isn't the full measure of what they do. They do for us in the spirit what Stevenson did for writers; they do what the Earlhams did for Burton; they do for us what Cameron Townsend ("Uncle Cam") did for the distribution of Bibles throughout the world in the languages of the world! I think Wordsworth says it well: "*What a great man accomplishes for the world is this: he does something that was never done before but which once it is done, becomes a standard for the rest of us, below which we can no longer be content.*"

O Lord of Love, in whom alone we live, kindle in our souls thy fire of love; give us to lay ourselves aside and to think of others as we kneel to thee. For those whom thou hast given us, dear to us as our own souls, thy best gift on earth, we ask thy blessing. If they are now far away, so that we cannot say loving words to them today, yet be thou near them, give them of thy joy, order their ways, keep them from sickness, from sorrow and from sin, and let all things bring them closer to thee. If they are near us, give us wisdom and grace to be true helpers of one another, serving in love's service all day long. Let nothing come between us to cloud our perfect trust, but help each to love more truly, more steadfastly, more unselfishly. Amen.

SAMUEL MCCOMB

4

Mission

Every preacher has his dream and this is mine; that not only will many of us ordinary men and women have this spirit of the cross in our common days but that there may be some special boy or girl, a youth of distinguished possibility, for whom God is particularly looking. When out into his generation such a youth moves, ready to do what nobody has any right to expect, the whole world is changed. O Youth like that, remember that the greatest things have not yet been done; the greatest music has not been composed; the greatest books have not been written; the greatest discoveries in science have not been made; the greatest advances in social life have not been achieved; the greatest triumphs of the spirit have not been won. They wait the coming of the right men and women, distinguished by a common characteristic—they yield obedience to the unenforceable laws!

HARRY E. FOSDICK

This one thing I do!

PAUL THE APOSTLE

I will learn his language and teach him about Jesus!

JOHN DUNCAN,
on his deathbed

I am come to do your will, O God.

I am the good shepherd. The good shepherd lays down his life for the sheep.

I have come, that they may have life, and have it to the full.

JESUS CHRIST

The People With The Power To See It Through Feel a Deep Sense Of . . .

Mission

The World Hater arrived in the world with his companions, Sin, Suffering and Death. He challenged man to combat, and from the first to the last he defeated them with ease. Some put up more of a fight than others, but they were no match for the World Hater and his grisly friends. And as their power grew, justice and mercy and goodness wilted and died. The planet groaned though it served Lord of Darkness. What they needed was a champion! But their champions were babes in contrast to this dark Warrior.

Then one day, from an obscure little village, a rumor began to spread. There was a young knight who had been preparing to challenge the Soul Destroyer. The planet hadn't chosen him, but he didn't care about that; he would champion their cause just the same. To the tournament he came, this glorious knight of God. And riding into the lists, with his head up, steady eyes and heart filled with courage, he rang his lance in confident challenge against the shields of Lord Foul, Sin, Suffering and Death! And the world held its breath as this gallant young lord suffered such powerful blows. Alone and unattended he fought, vulnerable and hurt he was, but he was obsessed and energized by his matchless task as he fought for his King's honor and mankind's freedom. And at great cost to himself he battered from their armored mounts the great enemies of those he loved. No wonder the cry went up in heaven: "Worthy art thou!"

And from the beginning (see Acts 2:23-42) as the word of this marvelous rescue was heralded, countless thousands rejoiced and streamed into the ranks of this young Lord's army. They didn't only find forgiveness, they found meaning, purpose and optimism. They were cheered by the fact that their new Lord had overcome the World. They were ecstatic that he called them to join him in bringing that message of freedom to all who hadn't heard. They were sobered by his word that they, like him, would endure pain, shame, times of fatigue and seeming loss. Some joined the young King's army of bright-eyed knights but found the cost not to their liking. They wanted the cheers but not the pain, the applause but not the price, the security but not the suffering. With sad eyes he watched them go back to the boredom of existence under the defeated lords of darkness. To the musty and damp kingdom of Rot, to life without thrills, direction or cause. With a sigh, he turns to face the sun while he calls to his troops: "It's time to be going. We have much yet to do for the world!"

Those who have the power to radiantly see it though have a deep sense of mission. And they don't think they called themselves; they believe they have been called!

One of my all-time favorite TV characters is "Captain

Freedom." He was one of the characters in the series "Hill St. Blues." He was a nut! He wore circus tights, a zip-up sweater, a cape, World War I flying helmet with goggles and tennis shoes. He was a crime fighter who often got in the way of the police. His only weapons were his presence, his verbal commands to "Stop this criminal act!" and his deep sense of mission! He ended his career when police were shooting it out with robbers. He jumped up on the hood of an automobile, held up his arms and commanded the robbers to "Stop this criminal act!" They shot him dead!

He was a nut, and nuts have nothing to offer this cynical world of pragmatists, but I loved him! I think mainly it was his innocence and his devotion to "the call" he felt. In dying he tells Mick that crime fighters like Mick and himself are the "thin line" between the evil world of crime and the vulnerable citizens. I keep noticing it's people who have a deep sense of mission, an all-consuming passion; it's those people who *give* their lives in service rather than rusting out in boredom!

These two crucial things go together in the lives of those who experience the power to see it through: (1) The conviction that they have been chosen, not by themselves, but by someone else, and (2) the conviction that what they have been called to is greater than themselves!

When Jesus looked the apostolic group in the eye and told them: "You did not choose me, I chose you . . ." (Jn. 15:16), he empowered them. Millions visited the Olympic Games in Los Angeles. They chose to be present, and it didn't matter very much whether they did or didn't. There were others at the Games who weren't self-chosen. They had been chosen by their *nation*, and it mattered a great deal whether or not they were there! And it makes a difference to how a man lives his life if he views himself as called by another or self-chosen. There's a sense of "perhaps I will, perhaps I won't" in the one and a sense of "I'm being depended on" in the other, and this second situation adds power to our endeavors.

Since the Reformation there has been a great deal of emphasis on the "personal" response in religion as opposed to "inheriting" a religious status. I'm not wishing to deny the need for proclaiming this. Just the same, in practice, if not in theory, the "calledness" has often been minimized if only by default.

The Bible is not only full of verses which expressly speak of God calling us, it is full of the notion. It is woven into the very texture of the Scriptures. Individual verses only bring into focus what the Bible teaches from beginning to end—the initiative is always of God!

"Abide in the same calling wherein he was *called*." "Preserved in Jesus Christ, and *called*: . . ." "Even as ye are *called* in one hope of your *calling*." "Worthy of God, who hath *called* you. . . ." "Faithful is he that *calleth* you, . . ." "God hath from the beginning chosen you. . . ." (KJV; emphasis mine). (I quickly counted forty times in the New Testament that this kind of thing is said—there are more!) It isn't the Christian's response which gets the emphasis in the New Testament; it is *the call* by God which gets the stress. Our stress on "personal choice" has its dangers. If we aren't careful, the individual's choice gains the center of the stage; *he* becomes the central character and a one-sidedness comes into our thinking and responding. The truth of John 15:16 is true for all of us in all ages: "You did not choose me, I chose you. . . ."

(But isn't it an amazing thing that Christ has this kind of confidence is us?) Gossip is rightly stunned by it. He says this about John 15:16 and the truth it tells:

> That surely, is the last and crowning wonder that leaves one staring with minds dazed and stunned. For it is not, you see, that you came

> upon Jesus Christ, and that your heart, stormed by the sheen and splendor. . . . all that would have been natural enough. But it was not that. He it was who came on you, turned and looked after you, said, There is a man to whom my heart is drawn, and out of whom I know I can fashion something of eternal value . . . . All Jericho was a tumult of welcome. Yet Christ who had so little to encourage him, was not much helped by that noisy enthusiasm, kept looking as he passed along the eager, crowding, shouting streets for something deeper, something better, something more, till his eyes, at long last, lit upon a face and stayed, seeing in it what he was seeking (Zaccheus).

We didn't just wake up one morning and decide, out of the blue, to become Christ's. The song writer was correct when she wrote: "He called me long before I heard, before my sinful heart was stirred; . . ." For some of us it was many years before we heard the voice of Christ calling us to follow him. But when we finally heard him, it wasn't ourselves we heard! It was *his* voice (Rom. 10:14, 17). When we said *yes* to Christ, it was to One who had already been calling us. Our salvation and calling wasn't *our* idea; it was *his* from beginning to end!

The next time you look in a mirror, remind yourself: "I have been chosen by Christ!" Let that truth sink in. Let the thought of Christ's greatness make that call as grand as it really is. To doubt Christ's call of us is to place more faith in ourselves than in him. It's to say: "He can't have chosen me!" when Jesus Christ says: "I have chosen you!"

It is this profound sense of *mission* that drove *Rabbi Duncan*. On his deathbed, the old man was told that a foreign sailor had been brought into the hospital and no one could understand him. The old man raised himself up and said, "I will learn his language and teach him about Jesus!" It's what drove *Francis Xavier* from a well-paid and much-sought post as lecturer in a university to the Far East to preach his faith. He rarely slept more than four hours; he'd hire himself out as a deckhand on ships and spend the night preaching to the lookout in the crow's nest. He's credited with bringing more than a million people into the Roman Catholic faith. He died of fever on a tiny Sancian island anxiously waiting permission to enter China so he could evangelize.

And that's what drove one philosophy professor to what used to be known as the Belgian Congo. A Paris missionary society's magazine caught his eye as he was about to throw it into the wastepaper basket. He read it and that night wrote in his diary: "My search is over!" Schweitzer took his three doctors' degrees (in theology, music and medicine) and wore himself out in service of the impoverished people of central Africa.

But isn't it amazing what some people give themselves to? I read recently that one Bible scholar finally completed his major contribution to helping us appreciate better the Good Book: He counted the word "and" in both Testaments (there are 46,227 occurrences). The *Peterborough Daily Telegraph* for June 2, 1988, carried the story. (Ah, well, at least he single-mindedly pursued *something* to a conclusion.)

It isn't enough to devote oneself to some cause or other. Since we only have one life, it's important that we make it count! It's perfectly legitimate to choose to be "a small cog in a large machine" if that machine has some real significance. We don't all have to be out front leading the parade. But surely we must set our sights on what really makes a difference for God and man.

Didn't Jesus talk about "weightier matters" of the

law?! Isn't there a danger in our being engrossed in narrow duties and small issues while vast needs stare us in the face? Isn't that precisely what Jesus accused these preachers of in Matthew 23:23? Must we go on forever paying lip service to the grandeur of the Cross while frittering our lives away in counting "ands" in the English Bible or things equivalent to that?

We need Someone to take from us the thousands of scattered little loyalties and send deep into our beings an all-consuming drive. The passion of Lincoln's life could be summed up in a sentence. And Paul's life has been understandably summed up by one man in the phrase: For Christ! John R. Mott's work in life was summed up in his slogan: "Jesus Christ to the nations in this generation!" What is it that possesses us?

There is no greatness in any man, it's been said, in whose heart there does not burn one grand, all-encompassing purpose which drives him even at awful cost to say, "I must!" When the Japanese bacteriologist, Hideyo Noguchi, was preparing to leave for Africa to see what he could do about yellow fever which was murdering hosts of people, he was reminded that it was dangerous and could cost him his life. He said: "Yes, I know, but I must!" He died of it! Here was a man who had already established his reputation with his work on syphilis and Oroya fever. Shouldn't he have sat back and taken his ease? He *couldn't*, so he "threw away" his life at the age of fifty-one. *He was driven!*

To redeem men from disease, ignorance, poverty and oppression, men and women have worn themselves out. Men and women, I mean, who made no confession of Jesus Christ but who had been seized by the spirit that Jesus himself would have been pleased with. And others, in the name of Christ, have gone to die in war zones while ministering to the needs of the victims of warmongers. There was the head doctor of a large hospital in China who was *driven* to make his one life count in the service of men. When the communist wing of the nationalist army came through, utterly destroying the hospital and scattering the patients, he grabbed as many instruments as was practical and followed those soldiers so that he could minister to them! *He was driven!*

There was once a carpenter who wanted to save this big, round crowded world—he, all alone! And God asked him: "Are you willing to pay the price? To leave home and all the quietness and peace of it for the tumult, tension and noise?" The serious young man, replied: "I am!" Some time passed and the crowds who first flocked to listen to him had begun to drift away, even to mock and scowl at him. "And are you still willing to go on?" God asked him. "Yes, I am!" he quietly said.

And later still when the crowds had grown hostile and the people he came to save began offering abuse and threats, when they used him when they needed him and dismissed him when they felt like it, God spoke to him. "And do you dare go on?" inquired God, his whole being glowing with admiration at the bravery of it all. And the young man said: "I do!"

Then one day the ugly shadow of a cross fell across his path. They took him, nailed him down and left him to die with nothing at all accomplished and without a single person really knowing what he had come for. And God gouged him, deep, with: "And are you willing to pay the full price?" The young man, dying, said: "Yes, Father!" Now, *that* is a strong sense of mission! *That* is what it means to be *driven*!

And all who have the power to see it through, to live devotedly and significantly, whatever their place or station in life, they all have that sense of mission, that sense of "calledness." They're all caught up in a cause they feel is greater than their own rights or comforts.

O God with steadfast heart, make us like thyself. Fill us with the power of a single purpose. Deliver us from a thousand scattered little loyalties and make us like Him whose solitary purpose was to do thy will in the loving rescue of a wayward humanity. Forbid us to be at the mercy of a multitude of little voices making demands on our time with trivial pursuits. Bless us with wisdom to know the difference between the weightier matters of the law and the narrow duties. Enable us not only to recognize but to seek above all, the kingdom of God and thy righteousness. Bless our resolve with kindness lest we run roughshod over bewildered but honest hearts who have not yet found their place in life with thee. But do thou bless us with a sweet ruthlessness that we will with conscience clear sweep aside the hindering trivia and do the King's business. In the name of Jesus we pray. Amen.

5

Sinfulness

Before reconciliation with God, the feeling of guilt is purely disabling. . . . later, as an undertone of felt unworthiness, it aids in fostering that humility and receptiveness apart from which the life of God cannot be ours.

H. R. MACKINTOSH

Christ Jesus came into the world to save sinners—of whom I am the worst. But for that very reason I was shown mercy so that in me, the worst of sinners, Christ Jesus might display his unlimited patience as an example for those who would believe on him and receive eternal life.

PAUL THE APOSTLE

It is equally dangerous for man to know God without knowing his own wretchedness, as to know his own wretchedness without knowing the Redeemer who can cure him.

PASCAL

There was a time when I wouldn't admit what a sinner I was. But my dishonesty made me miserable and filled my days with frustration. All day and all night your heart was heavy on me. My strength evaporated like water on a sunny day until I finally admitted all my sins to you and stopped trying to hide them. I said to myself, "I will confess them to the Lord." And you forgave me! All my guilt is gone.

PSALM 32:3-5; LB

(There are only two groups of people) the righteous who believe themselves sinners; the rest, sinners who believe themselves righteous.

PASCAL

The People With The Power To See It Through Have Come To Terms With Their . . .

Sinfulness

Before I get involved in this discussion and forget to say it, let me say this now: *Sin loses!* Sin is bad, but it's beat! Sin is strong, but Christ in us is stronger! Sin is a usurper and a thief, and we are to resist it from the cradle to the grave! Greater is he that is in us (or wants to be in us) than he that is in the world (1 Jn. 4:4)!

Pascal in *Pensees* (168) makes this wise statement:

> It is equally dangerous for man to know God without knowing his own wretchedness, as to know his own wretchedness without knowing the Redeemer who can cure him.

We dare not tell the truth about Sin and leave people with the notion that they must handle it on their own. And we dare not tell people about the redeeming work of God in Christ without helping them to realize just what horror God saved them from.

We mustn't overstate the case about Sin's power lest we so dismay people that they quit the struggle against it. We mustn't understate the truth of Sin's power or people might think they can stroll into holiness with their hands in their pockets!

How are we helped when we recognize that Sin is a very powerful and deeply-rooted force in human lives?

It will keep our struggle against Sin from becoming casual! When we give people the impression that Sin is something we can peel off (like a sweater in a warm room) just when we're ready, should it surprise us if they don't view it as a serious problem? If we teach them that Sin's roots go deep into us, wrapping themselves around our souls, then the battle against Sin will be carried on in grim determination.

It will keep us from deep depression when we discover Sin is tough to beat! Give people the idea that Sin is easy to beat and when they find it an enemy that will not let them go, depression can set in. ("Why can't I beat it?" becomes a major question.) But teach people that Sin is a tough, durable and very powerful enemy, and they won't expect an easy victory. They'll be able to live with defeats without drifting into despair.

It will keep us from self-loathing and self-despising which weaken our resolve to become holy. If a man is encouraged to believe that Sin can be easily defeated and then finds himself in a life-and-death struggle with it, self-loathing becomes prominent. "Everyone else is beating this thing, why can't I?" enters his mind. "I must be pathetically weak! I must be destitute of character!" There aren't many things more paralyzing than self-despising. It isn't a useful emotion, and its presence retards our spiritual growth. But teach men that Sin is a savage and very powerful enemy, and every victory against Sin is gratefully noted. Every loss is sadly acknowledged, but losses are (in a healthy sense) expected!

It will keep us from believing that we're "not trying" when we still experience awful struggles against Sin. Deny or underestimate Sin's awful power and alarming nature, and people who struggle with Sin begin to think they mustn't be trying. After all, if they were really trying, the struggle would be over in a relatively short time. That's the impression people get who underestimate Sin's power and rootedness! And if we're not trying, remember, "Christ doesn't want us"! Try struggling against Sin with that kind of doubt eating away at your mind! But teach people that Sin has taken root deep in our being, and our endless struggle against Sin will not suggest to us that we "aren't trying."

It will keep us from becoming irritated/angry/impatient with those who aren't making the progress against Sin we think they should make (and which we think we're making). People who have a shallow view of Sin's power and rootedness often become "righteous snobs." Luke 18:9 speaks of those who "trusted in themselves and despised others" (KJV). They can't understand why others aren't as good as they are. They find it quite easy (with some effort, of course) to be decent and upright. And so: "If I'm able to do it with some effort, so can they!" seems to be their view of things. "If they aren't decent and upright like me, it's because they aren't really trying, and I'm a cut above them!" seems a logical conclusion. Well, we've all had some grasp of the truth that evil is evil, but it took Jesus to really make it clear that decency and uprightness can be evil too!

It will help us to better appreciate the marvelous character of our salvation! Have you ever had a close encounter with death? One which you didn't really think as "close" when it happened? Later it really came home to you how very close it had been? Your heart lurched like an old generator kicking on, and your pulse zipped up to a hundred? It's something like that when we underestimate the truly alarming nature of Sin. We know that God saved us. Yes, and we know we're grateful for that. But after all, our condition wasn't *that* perilous, so while we want to be grateful there's no need to fall to our knees in adoring gratitude. Listen, Sin was *feeding* on us, like some repulsive parasite, gorging itself on our very being; we were being digested; our being was being sucked from us! Some "wise" old men tell us there's nothing to worry about, but *something is feeding on mankind*!

The wondrous character of our salvation doesn't end there. Our salvation is an *ongoing* salvation! God has not only "saved" us, he is "saving" us. A mature (but still imperfect) grasp of the awful evil and power of Sin will lead us to breathlessly and tremblingly thank God not only for bringing us initially into Christ for salvation but for his ongoing grace and power that keeps us in Christ without whom there is no safety from this godforsaken power.

The Reality of Sin

Ten minutes with a newspaper or a television shows the reality of Sin! A serious self-examination tells you how real Sin is. Some tell us we do evil because of our genes. We hate, kill, despise and brutalize because our brains are programmed that way. Others tell us we're evil due to our evolutionary background. Our violent and selfish ways were useful when we were fighting our way up; we simply haven't outgrown those traits which were useful to us at one point in our history. Others are sure it's our childhood (and present) environment that explains all of our evil. Some say it was all Adam's fault, and others insist that God himself is to blame. Well, *however we explain it, everyone knows there's something to explain!* Evil is real! Most psychologists used to spend a lot of their time telling people "sin" was an invention of the church to keep people in line. That message isn't as popular as it used to be. Many psychologists and psychiatrists now see that no one is being helped by this. They're seeing that there is a dark stain in man that must be recognized as really existing! (Freud himself had nothing good to say about Man.)

The Universality of Sin

Romans 3:10 tells us: "None is righteous, no, not one!"(RSV). Romans 3:23 says: "All have sinned and fall short of the glory of God!" (RSV). Pascal correctly assures us that there is only one group of sinners divided into two: "The righteous who believe themselves sinners; the rest, sinners who believe themselves righteous."

The Many Faces of Sin

Listen to this from Harry E. Fosdick:

> Sometimes sin is gross and terrible. It staggers down the street; it blasphemes with oaths that can be heard; it wallows in vice unmentionable by modest lips. Then prosperity visits sin. It moves to a finer residence; it seeks the suburbs or gets itself housed on a college campus. It changes all its clothes. It is no longer indecent and obscene; its speech is mild; its civility is irreproachable. But at heart it is the same old sin, self-indulgent, callous,

envious, cruel, unclean. As anybody may easily observe, sin takes on a very high polish.

That's true, isn't it?!

Sin shows itself in verbal obscenity *and* flattery and gossip! It shows itself in drug addiction (booze included) *and* craving for praise! It is seen in open tyranny *and* self-promotion! It's there in flagrant cruelty *and* self-righteousness! Sin shows itself in disgusting racism *and* in religious sectarianism! There are sins of the *flesh* like lust, gluttony and drunkenness. But there are sins of the temperament like bitterness, sulkiness and irritability. There are sins in the area of social attitudes like racism and radical nationalism, and there are sins of the self-centered such as Christ scathed in Luke 10:31-32 and 12:21.

But we need to go further than that. Sin doesn't only show itself in gross evils as distinct from sophisticated evils, it shows itself in *gross evils* and *pathetic lives*. The most common word for Sin in the New Testament is one which means to "miss the mark" or "fall short."

Christ came into the world, said someone, not so much to convict us of our transgressions as to convict us of our possibilities!

Sin shows itself in a *narrow heart*. A life that is frittered away in narrow duties while vast needs are staring us in the face. Christ wasn't very interested in "blamelessness" or a "careful avoidance of evil." He saw our lives as empty and wasted (see 1 Pet. 1:18). He watches us spend them on trivial things, worrying over incidentals, weeping over tiny losses and fragmenting over small disappointments.

The Master sees us substituting occasional prayers, church-going and decency for lives filled with redemptive passion like his own! In this we are *sinful*! We are nice people who associate with other nice people who sing nice songs in one another's nice presence to a nice God who wants us all to be nicer. In this we are *sinful*! It is sinful to settle for less than we've been created for! Passionless lives are sinful! There is no greatness in a life that is fragmented into a thousand little loyalties and which lacks one grand passion! A life that can view the world's awful need of redemption and turn to serve its own decent pursuits is unlike Christ, and however decent it is, it is *sinful* at the core! *There is none righteous, no not one!*

The Depth, Power and Rootedness of Sin

We don't need to tell lies about Man to insist that he is depraved! Jeremiah, astonished at the evil of his people, proclaims the word of God and says: "The heart is deceitful above all things and beyond cure. Who can understand it?" (Jer. 17:9). Only God can (Jer. 17:10). The "heart" is used in various ways in the Bible, but in the Old Testament it usually speaks of Man's "control center," the core of his being, out of which everything issues.

God in Genesis 8:21 had this word about the heart: "I will never again curse the ground because of man, for the imagination of man's heart is evil from his youth" (RSV).

And Jesus had this to say in Mark 7:21-23 about Man's heart: "For from within, out of men's hearts, come evil thoughts, sexual immorality, theft, murder, adultery, greed, malice, deceit, lewdness, envy, slander, arrogance and folly. All these evils come from inside and make a man 'unclean.' "

It isn't just that Man's deeds are evil, his heart is evil! It isn't just that he does wrong things, his life's direction is bent! *Sin isn't an essential part of Man's nature, but it has diverted the flow of his life away from God and his fellow-man so that he dishonors God, his neighbor and himself!* Man has been twisted at the center of his being, and as Ramm correctly notes, he issues evil edicts because he is bent at "mission control." (*This* is what God has saved us from and what he goes on saving us from.)

As I understand the Scriptures and life, in the beginning we were sinners because we sinned. By and by, we sinned because we're sinners, and that's our condition today. We don't have to believe in a badly stated "total" depravity to accept the Bible's witness of our deep and pervasive depravity.

The historian Herbert Butterfield insists that *history* proclaims a clear message: No matter how good the scheme for human betterment is, it will be undermined by the evil of people. Jung, the psychoanalyst, in a frank statement, said: "We stand perplexed and stupified before the phenomena of Nazism or Bolshevism because we know nothing about man . . . we stand face to face with the terrible questions of evil and do not even know what is before us, let alone what is against us." Doesn't this echo Jeremiah 17:9?! Franz Kafka tersely commented: In a conflict between you and the world, bet on the world!

Everything we touch is turned to evil. Medical advances are used to butcher millions of babies in "abortions on demand." Scientific discoveries are used to create nuclear, chemical and bacteriological bombs. Our airplanes are made into bombers, our moving vehicles are made into tanks, our photographic expertise is turned to pornographic filth, our newly discovered ways of perfecting crop production are used to exploit the vulnerable nations.

But this kind of talk, though altogether true, can so easily promote self-righteousness among the decent and religious people. It can easily result in our feeling that "they" are terribly evil and we "used to have trouble with sin." It's awfully hard for upright people to see themselves as sin-smitten.

In one of the *Peanuts* cartoons, Charlie Brown lectures Lucy who is admiring herself in a mirror. "And, besides, never forget that beauty is only skin deep!" Lucy turns on him, yelling: "*I deny* that! My beauty is not only on the surface, it goes down deep . . . layer after layer! Yes, sir (she says with a scornful look), I have very *thick* beauty!" Decent people need convicted too. If their lives are generally respectable, their behavioral patterns within acceptable limits and if their thoughts seldom or never stray into "fleshly" areas, it's difficult for them to think they suffer from the same "disease" as the rest of the world. They find it hard to *really* believe the old saying: "There but for the grace of God go I!" (I suggest at this point you read again the sections on "the many faces of sin" and "why it is that many don't make it.")

C. S. Lewis in the *Narnia Chronicles* (volume 6) tells how Edmund, a spoiled little brat, finds a dragon cave. In it there is treasure beyond his wildest dreams. He begins to think greedy, dragonish thoughts, falls asleep and awakens to find he is what he thought—a dragon. Only Aslan, the lion, can free him from this awful predicament. Edmund washes and the dragon skin comes off . . . but there's another underneath. He washes again, the skin comes off . . . but there's yet another. Finally the lion rips at him with his awful sharp claws. Edmund is pained deep in the center of his being but . . . underneath, he is fresh and clean; he's new again. Lewis was trying to tell us that the "dragonish nature" isn't easily dispensed with!

The ancient Greeks told of Heracles (Hercules) saving his wife from the unwanted attentions of Nessus, the centaur. From a great way off Heracles put an arrow in the rapacious centaur who caught some of his own blood in a little bottle. "Wash your husband's shirt in this," said the wounded Nessus, "and you'll have no more trouble with him running after other women." Heracles' wife didn't realize there was hydra poison in the blood of Nessus. Later she washed the strong man's shirt in it and sent it with her servant to give to Hercules when he was to offer up a sacrifice to the gods. The shirt, like acid, burned into him. He tried to tug it off and it wouldn't come off. He dragged it off, and with it he dragged off his flesh until he died.

He is blinded who thinks that Sin is easily stripped off! Our theology of Sin is shallow indeed if we think that God saves us from something which can be defeated by a few prayers, church attendance, vows and resolutions! If Romans 7 teaches us anything, it teaches us that human knowledge, human diagnosis and human resolve can't master Sin! It doesn't annihilate the problem just to *know* we have one! It doesn't rid us of our "disease" because we're capable of diagnosing and understanding it. And resolving not to do evil hasn't helped one of us in all history to keep from sinning! (With the exception of our blessed Redeemer, we've all groveled and drunk from a stagnant pool. And God help us, we slake our evil thirsts at them yet!) Did we think the "Prince of this world" became the Lord of Darkness without great power? "Did we in our own strength confide, the battle would be losing!" cried Luther, never more right than then! And whether he's a Christian or not, a man's a fool who thinks: "I used to have trouble with Sin, but I'm over it now!" (*See Galatians 5:17!*) There'll be no "I'm over it now" until a better day dawns hereafter. Until then, if God in his grace does not ongoingly save us from Sin, we'll never see his face!

Given that a man is sensitive to the holiness of God seen in the life and death of Jesus Christ, his own heart condemns him as totally unfit for God's company. We feel this even when we're in the presence of some devoted man or woman of God. They intimidate us into silence by their very air, the sanctity that seems to exude from them. Their devotion and sacrifice make us feel our awful and ingrained selfishness. We're so uncomfortable in their presence and yet drawn to them.

It is mysteriously easy, said one writer, for the morally earnest man to grow proud of himself. But if we are ever, as sensitive people, to enjoy a warm and honorable relationship with God as his children, all self-satisfaction must be torn out by the roots!

Think about it! Some of the simplest experiences reveal what we are at a deeper level than our well-controlled behavior would suggest. Our first reaction to a piece of bitter criticism from somebody we don't like especially well is something like resentment. The first emotion we feel at the success of an unpleasant rival is envy. Yes, of course, we may well suppress the resentment or envy and may even manage a nobler response to it all a little later, but there it was! If we faced the truth we would learn things about ourselves. By strong "self-discipline" we can keep these things in check and train ourselves into decent outward behavior in the company of our peers. Just the same, the "flesh" is alive and well!

The trouble with many of us is that we're not subjected to a lot of sustained "stress" *without a lot of moral support from the host of friends around us.* If we're pained by some injustice, we have lots of loved ones to help us bear the burden and smother the pain. We have props all around us, holding us together. If the props were taken away and we had to face even small injustices on our own, we'd get a better picture of ourselves. So, *because* of those who surround us and *with the help of* those around us, we can suppress the inner evil impulses which blaze up in spite of years of suppression.

When God comes telling us to love even our *enemies,* we either surround ourselves with *friends* or excuse ourselves as being "only human." In either case we evade the real picture. What God calls for is worlds away from our actual condition. The free-flowing and glad-hearted love of God and our neighbor (our enemy) exists in spurts and trickles. Our "love-pool" is dried up when even a few people seriously slake their thirst at it. Our eagerness to serve is short-circuited immediately if we begin to think we're being "taken for granted" or "used." We may continue to do serving things, but the heart is gone. We keep going because we don't want people to know we're sulking or feel unappreciated.

We must stop comparing ourselves with others whose outward behavior is poorer than our own. We must stop assessing ourselves merely by well-controlled behavioral patterns. We must begin to get a glimpse of our heart and the awful corruption that exists in there along with the better elements. Until we do that we're only pretending to know ourselves; until we do that, it's only the crust, the veneer we're dealing with. And when the truth of all this dawns on us, *it is all over with self-satisfaction!* At that point, one of two things must happen—either we sink in ruin or we sink to our knees in desperate need, confessing to God that we've repented with a repentance which needs repented of!

Some years ago a number of us went to a cafeteria to eat and to discuss ways and means to help our students better serve the unforgiven. We were anxious to excite them about mission work in foreign fields. How do we help them to surrender their rights, the security of home and the comforts of America? How could we inspire them to take their young families into uncertainty, loneliness and primitive conditions for Christ's sake? This was the purpose of our being together.

We chose a nonsmoking section. We were eating and talking as we ate about this noble enterprise. Then we noticed there was smoke in the air. Several ladies had sat down at the table next to ours and had taken to smoking. It was at that point the murmuring began. We were growling and scowling, muttering and moaning. We all contributed to the rising swell of indignation. One of the ladies heard what I said, looked up and for the first time saw the large "No Smoking" sign and immediately put out the cigarette. She leaned over and apologized to me. I was utterly crushed! Her spirit was so good and mine (which was typical of us all) was gutless and whining. I was *so* embarrassed I hadn't the strength to say to the lady: "No, ma'am, you shouldn't apologize to me. I need to apologize to you for all of us sitting here!"

I wonder what she would have thought if I had then told her why we were meeting in Furr's Cafeteria? I wonder how far I would have gotten with her had I then began to share Christ with her? I wonder what the students would have thought had they been invisible observers of it all? I don't wonder *at all* what God thought of our pathetic exhibition. I don't remember another thing that was said at our table that day, but I do know I went back to the classroom and the students with more to think about than how I was going to verbalize their need to practice self-sacrifice. I'm ashamed of that incident! But it's one of many I can tell you about. There are many others I couldn't confess.

God Insists That We Shoulder The Blame for Our Sin

He does that because there can be no life with him and no forgiveness without our doing that!

First John 1:8-10 tells us plainly that if we refuse to acknowledge our sinfulness we make God out to be a liar; that his word has no place in us and that we don't give truth a place to live in us! The passage insists that we *confess* so that we can have both fellowship with and forgiveness from God!

Confession involves: (1) an acknowledgement that sin exists; (2) that we have actually sinned; (3) that we are responsible for our sinning; (4) that God has been grieved and dishonored; (5) a renunciation of sin; (6) a purpose toward obedience; and (7) a trusting of ourselves to grace. For John, *confession* is equivalent to a full-bodied repentance.

One cannot believe in the forgiveness of sins unless he believes in *confession*. If there's nothing to confess, there's nothing to forgive. Not only do we not forgive an innocent person, we *cannot*! You cannot *forgive* a boy for beating your boy if that boy didn't beat your boy! When we *confess*, we honor God. If we deny the need for *confession*, we deny the need for Christ's death and make him appear to be a deluded young fool for thinking he needed to redeem us!

Our tendency to blame God or others for our sinfulness is seen as early as Adam in Genesis 3:12. But after all is said about the difficulties of our environment (homelife and peer pressure), we know we're guilty! God knows full well that we aren't *exclusively* responsible for our wrongs and that some evils are more evil than others (see Mt. 11:22, 24; Ezek. 16:47-52). But after all allowances are made, God stamps across mankind: *There is none righteous, no not one!* And in our fairer moments we know there were times when we said *yes* and could/should have said *no*! There were times when we could/should have said *yes* and we said *no*. And God insists that we acknowledge that if we want life with and forgiveness from him!

God insists that we shoulder the blame for our sin because without that there can be no peace or assurance that life with him is ours to enjoy!

Browning, the famous poet, had friends who kept

trying to assure him that he wasn't as evil as he thought himself to be. Then he said he met up with Christ. Christ told him, said Browning: "Browning, you are worse than you ever dreamed you were!" Strangely enough, the poet said, that didn't depress him; it gave him hope! If Christ's assessment of him was both plainly honest and stunningly accurate, then his promises to the poet could be received with assurance!

God is no "divine dupe" who sees only the best in Man, who doesn't know the awful evil in Man. (You've come across parents like this, haven't you?! Who cannot believe their child would "do a thing like that." Didn't they make you feel ill?!)

Knowing that God knows our evil all the way down to its roots in our very being brings us comfort. If knowing all that, he still offers us life, forgiveness and a place of work at his side, we can joyfully fight the good fight. There never will come a day, says Gossip, when God will say to us: "Well, my gifts aren't for people like you. I didn't realize that you would be this stupid or this evil." No new and sinister facts will come to light about us that will make him change his mind about us.

This is why the Christ forces Peter (Jn. 21) to confess three times what he denied three times. *Of course*, it was painful for Peter, but from that time forward he didn't need to worry if his weakness would lead Christ to distrust him. Knowing him to the core of his being, Jesus still commissioned Peter to "feed my sheep"! Knowing that God fully knows the depth of our Sin allows us peace.

The Essential Nature of Sin

The single human response sought by God is for us to love (first God and then our neighbor). Therefore, the central nature of Sin is *lovelessness*! Since love works no ill to the neighbor, the presence of love excludes the presence of Sin in our response to him. The presence of Sin means the absence of love (Rom. 13:8-10 with Gal. 5:14). And the absence of love, says Paul in 1 Corinthians 13, makes vice out of virtue.

Tear off all the masks that Sin wears, and you'll find lovelessness staring at you! Analyze every lovely and gallant virtue, and at its core you'll find love of God and neighbor. To the degree that love is absent, to that degree Sin is present. To the degree that love is being expressed toward God and man, to that degree Sin is banished!

Don't be afraid of this kind of talk. Don't let the "Hollywood treatment" of the word *love* drive you from it. It's a bad mistake to allow the world to take precious and rich words from us. Don't avoid the word; rightly define it; correctly illustrate it; fully develop it. Give it its full biblical connotation. *Love* is a "community" word; it is experienced only in fellowship with others. *Selfishness* (with all that that involves, like self-exaltation, self-service, self-promotion, and the like) is only lovelessness spelled another way. The essence of Sin is lovelessness, the selfish withholding of ourselves from rich harmonious fellowship with God and one another.

How Can We Enjoy Life With God While Sinners?

Seek forgiveness because sensitive souls are tortured by sin that isn't forgiven! Listen to this from David:

> Blessed is he whose transgressions are forgiven, whose sins are covered. Blessed is the man whose sin the Lord does not count against him and in whose spirit there is no

> deceit. When I kept silent, my bones wasted away through my groaning all day long. For day and night your hand was heavy upon me; my strength was sapped as in the heat of summer. Then I acknowledged my sin to you and did not cover up my iniquity. I said, "I will confess my transgressions to the Lord"—and you forgave the guilt of my sin.
>
> Therefore let everyone who is godly pray to you while you may be found; surely when the mighty waters rise, they will not reach him. You are my hiding place; you will protect me from trouble and surround me with songs of deliverance (Ps. 32:1-7).

Until he sought and found forgiveness with God, David was miserable. As long as he refused to confess it, to come to an honest renunciation of it, he wasted away. I suspect all of us have felt that at one time or another.

When the famous Samuel Johnson was a boy, his father had a stall at the open market in Uttoxeter. One day he asked Samuel to come and help him there. The boy was too proud to do such a humble thing and stoutly refused to do it. More than sixty years later, when Johnson was now firmly established as one of the giants of the literary world, that pride and rebellion still ate at his sensitive heart. So he went to the market, close to the very spot where the stall had been, and for more than thirty hours he stood bareheaded in the rain. This old, famous and dignified man stood there seeking peace after more than sixty years. This "public penance" was Johnson's way to life and peace. I looked at this scene which is depicted in plaster on the side of what once was an old weigh station in the market square. And I thought Johnson must have felt what David felt, for he found peace only in the way David did!

When Michael Hebblethwaite was an old and honored man, he was tortured by the conviction that he hadn't been the brother he should have been to his younger brother. The younger man ended his life on a gallows. Hebblethwaite lived for many years with this torment. Finally he petitioned the prison authorities for the privilege to be buried in the gloomy prisonyard beside the bones of his dishonored brother. No rest, no peace, no life is there for us unless we come to face our sin and find forgiveness!

And do you remember Hawthorne's novel, *The Scarlet Letter*? Its setting is a puritan colony. Hester Prynne has been immoral. In due time her shame is visible, and the community punishes her by making a public exhibition of her. She will not only be placed in stocks, she will wear a scarlet letter "A" to proclaim her shame and be a warning to all others. She steadfastly refuses to name her fellow sinner. There will be sermons preached against immorality in the presence of the community while Hester is there in the center. The preacher will be the young, capable and well-loved Arthur Dimmesdale. The young, capable well-loved preacher *who is Hester's unknown partner in sin*! And Dimmesdale can find no rest! How will he rid himself of the crushing burden? He's intelligent—will he ease the burden by burying himself in theological pursuits? (But how can he think God's thoughts under these circumstances?) He's a capable preacher—will he inspire people to heroic lives for God? (But how can he inspire others to heroism while he is daily cowardly?) He is a servant—will he go humbly from door to door doing good and find peace in that? (But how can he find peace in that when such an evil is eating his heart away?) There is only one way to peace! He joins Hester in the stocks and finds forgiveness!

So much physical illness, so much emotional trauma, so much below-par life stems from unresolved guilt!

Dreams we should be dreaming, dreams we *want* to dream are turned away from the door of our souls by the guilt which tells us we "have no right" to dream such dreams! Unforgiven sin takes the enthusiasm out of our voices. We feel we have no right to denounce evil or praise a holy endeavor while we endure the torment of buried sin. Within us, like a bell buoy mournfully clanging with the rise of each swell, our unresolved guilt gongs out in never-ending tones the guilt which is feeding on us.

Get forgiveness!

Remember that God delights in forgiving sin! Micah 7:18-19 says this: "Who is a God like you, who pardons sins and forgives the transgression of the remnant of his inheritance? You do not stay angry forever but delight to show mercy. You will again have compassion on us; you will tread our sins underfoot and hurl all our iniquities into the depths of the sea."

To sensitive and penitent hearts, God generously pardons (Is. 55:7), and he is delighted with the opportunity to do it. That *is* what Micah says! And that *is* what Luke 15 teaches us from beginning to end.

I understand that the more sensitive the heart is the more difficulty it has in coming again and again for forgiveness. That's as it should be! Just the same, we've got to stop being so humble! To trust God means we trust his testimony about himself and he claims that it makes him rejoice when we penitently turn to him. So if we insist on living tormented lives because of unresolved guilt, let's do it without professing that God is slow to forgive us!

Recognize chastisement for what it is! This is a hard saying! It isn't especially hard to understand intellectually, but emotionally it's an awfully hard pill to swallow. Jacob, the cheater, is a parable for all of us who force God to use a "sweet violence" in our lives which leaves us limping and wounded for the rest of our lives. The desperate man (Gen. 32) rises from his wrestle with the angel, blessed but limping. When people saw him after that, they knew he had been beaten!

But chastisement is nothing to be ashamed of because it is a proof of God's love for us (Rev. 3:19). We're able to rejoice within because even though the wound reminds us of some deeds or traits we're thoroughly ashamed of and embarrassed by, it also reminds us that Someone cares enough to get our attention!

This is a very serious matter, and we need to get our thinking clear on it, says Dodds. When we suffer chastisement from God, we are not to lie flattened and whining in the dark as though God *didn't* care. We are not to think because we see no "limping" in others that he cares less for us than them. Such an absence of chastisement may have another message (Heb. 12:8). No, when we've been sorely beaten by God, we need to do what Jacob did when he felt the pain—cling even more tightly to him who gives us the wound. We need in the desperation of trust, to gain a blessing and a new status from the work of God on us.

We *must* remember that God went looking for Jacob at Jabbok *not* to do him harm but to bless him! God wasn't reluctant to bless Jacob—he *longed* to bless him! The need for doing violence to Jacob lay within Jacob, not God! *The same is true of all of us!* The severe mercies God brings our way is part of his ongoing work of saving us! God finds no joy in bringing grief to us (Lam. 3:33) and he doesn't want us to die under his surgery, but salvation is an *ongoing* process. There's more to being God's than simply being acquitted (justified), and God loves us too much to allow us to live like pigs. He loves us enough to share with us the pain he brings on us in order to ongoingly redeem and protect us. *Recognize chastisement as the love of God expressed to you in a severe mercy.*

View things from Christ's balanced perspective! Before I develop this point a little I need you to take note of this bald statement: *The disciple of Christ must steer clear of complacency and always pursue growth in Jesus Christ!* There now, I've said what every Christian has known since the day of their new birth.

There is a real problem in endlessly checking your own spiritual pulse and endlessly taking your spiritual temperature. To spend hours each day in front of a mirror searching for and examining defects in your appearance doesn't make a bit of sense. It makes no more sense to do it spiritually.

It is absolutely crucial that we spend more time thinking about what we're running to and less time thinking about what we're running from.

Wodrow, in his *Analecta*, says Frank Boreham, told of a Scottish minister who, once a year, would meet a girl at an inn owned by her father. Anxious to help the girl to come to Christ, the minister took every opportunity to speak to her about it. Before he left he was able to persuade this life-loving girl with the laughing eyes to pray each day before she went to bed. She was to ask God each night: "O Lord, show me myself!"

When he returned a year later, he was astonished by the change in her. All the sparkle and laughter was gone from her. The brightness had left her eyes and a fixed gloom had come on her spirit. As they talked she could speak of nothing but her wickedness, her faithlessness, her trivial life and her awful need. He tried in vain to get her to throw herself on the love and mercy of God because she felt that God's love couldn't be intended for the likes of her. But he managed to persuade her to pray a single prayer each night before retiring: It was this: "O Lord, show me thyself!" The following year when he saw her, he saw a transformed girl! She wasn't the roguish and frivolous girl he had first met, nor did she have the grim look of the last year. She was joyful, had a settled peace and was overflowing with gratitude. *The first prayer had kept her looking at herself; the second kept her looking at her Savior.*

This leads me then to say that Christ is not only willing to receive the little we can give—he's eager to do so!

It's part of our sinfulness not to honor Christ as we ought! It's also a part of our sinfulness that we won't give credit where it is due! Sensitive people are poor judges of themselves. They impatiently dismiss praise, they refuse to admit there is good in themselves as well as evil, they ridicule their own endeavors and scorn their progress in Christ as paltry. *Such a spirit isn't good!*

Hebrews 6:10 is a word from God we need to pay attention to. God knows very well how evil we are, but that doesn't keep the writer from reminding us: "God is not unfair; he will not forget what you have done, nor the love you have shown for his sake. . . ." (Moffatt). There's a lot we need to learn from this. *God is fair; he isn't one-sided!* In the course of rebuking these Hebrews for numerous things, God makes it clear he doesn't only see their evil, he has noted their service for his name. God teaches us here something about his own approach to struggling people. "I would regard it as unfair of me," he tells them, "if I simply dismissed all the good work you have done for my sake!" *Don't be holier than God! Don't be more demanding than God!* Try looking at God's servants as generously as God does. Even if that servant turns out to be you!

Christ is so eager to receive the little we give him! Don't you remember how openly he expresses his astonishment at the centurion's faith in Luke 7?! Don't you recall how, on the very night he was to be betrayed, while the disciples were arguing over who was number one, Jesus bragged on them (Lk. 22:24-28)?! He bigheartedly and truthfully said: "You are those who have stood by me in my trials!" (Lk. 22:28). He saw beyond their selfishness and their evil to what they did and what they would have done if they could have. And he credited that to them and forgave the rest! *Are you aware that Christ is like that?*

McGinnis tells us that Adélie penguins in the Antarctic have a lovely courting ritual. The male penguin brings his lady a gift. In that part of the world there is no Neiman-Marcus and not a great selection of gifts. The boy waddles down to the beach and searches among the stones until he finds a smooth stone he really likes. He waddles back up to his lady and humbly lays it at her feet. And she joyfully accepts it. (Is it too much to imagine her glancing around at the onlooking girls with that "He's such a little pet" look? It is? Ah well, I just had to ask.)

God has always been "grateful." Isn't that amazing?! In a world absolutely filled with wickedness, he sees the bravery of one man (Gen. 7:1). That man is quite capable of sin (Gen. 9:21), but God glows with admiration at his doing what he could do.

I think it was Anatole France who told the story of the juggler and the statue of Christ. The juggler had been part of a circus before he entered monastic life. He wasn't good at language studies or prayers; in fact he didn't have much to offer in any area of monastery life. One day he stopped in front of a statue of Christ, wanting to do something for him but unable to think of anything suitable. So he began to juggle and do acrobatics. When he was finished, sweating and breathless, he reverently nodded to Christ. This became a regular habit. Some of his fellow monks saw this and complained to the head of the monastery. Together they all watched the man perform and then reverently bow his head. As they watched him disappear down the corridor they saw, says France, the head of the statue turn to look after the juggler and smile! Yes, I know about the limitations of the story, but I love it! It's just like the living Christ to do such a thing!

Don't whitewash your evil, and don't trumpet your lovely deeds for Christ. But don't forever sit in judgment on yourself. We don't make really good servants of Christ because we are sinful. But that same sinfulness keeps us from being good judges. Sin has jaundiced our judgment as well as our service! *God doesn't hold us guilty for not being God, so let's be fair—even with ourselves (Heb. 6:10).*

Trust Christ's ability to transform lives! At this point I'd suggest you look again at the chapter on "Hope." Listen, if Christ doesn't have the power to transform a willing heart into his own likeness, we have no gospel at all! We want forgiveness (and God knows we need it!), but we want a holy freedom, a noble power, an energy to carry out our lovely intentions. Christ assures us that he will not only forgive us but that he will cure us! Read 1 Thessalonians 5:23-24, drink it in and let the hope stir within you. Take God at his word, why don't you!

We see God changing people all around us. There are times when we're almost awed by the transformation we see in the life of a notorious brute that we've known personally. We read about these changes; we hear about these changes; we even watch such changes—when will we believe that God can and will do that to us? *It's none of our business how long it takes or how painful the process!* Do you want it? Are you (by his grace) cooperating as much as you're able? Yes?! Then, unless he's faithless, you will gain the victory over evil in your life! And God cannot be faithless (2 Tim. 2:13)!

Matthew had sold himself to Rome in becoming a tax collector. Day after day he sat there hated and (perhaps) hating. Enduring the scorn, the obscenities, the loss of fellowship. Arthur Gossip imagines the talk that must have gone on around the corners when the rumor circulated that the new rabbi in town had called Matthew to be one of his apostles. "You'll never guess who he called!" someone chuckles. "No, no, better than that! I hear he's called Matthew! Yes, Matthew—old 'Money Bags' himself. And he was serious, they say. Walked right up to him and told him he was to leave all and follow him. Leave all his money and his soft job? It'll be a winter day in July when that miser does that!" And with lots of jeers and laughs they would have broken up. But the jeers would have turned to awe and the chuckles to astonished unbelief when the word got around that Levi *had* gone after Christ!

There it was all the time in Matthew, and only Christ saw it! Behind the bitter look, underneath the greedy hands, hidden under the layers of selfishness was a soul crying for challenge and change! Well?

How Can We Help People Struggling Against Sin?

We need to acknowledge that this is what we have been called to do for Christ! Bonhoeffer reminds us that "the law of Christ" is a "bearing" law (Gal. 6:2). We have been called to become strong so that we can bear the infirmities of the weak (Rom. 15:1-3; 2 Cor. 11:29). A soldier is no less a dedicated foe of the enemy because he takes time to save a wounded comrade from dying of his wounds.

We must never whitewash the evil we see in people, even if they are our friends. Maybe, *especially* if they're our friends. We don't have to brutalize people in order to confront them with their evil. We don't even have to be rude or impassive. We only have to try a little harder to do this well, and by God's grace we'll do it. (See Gal. 6:1.)

It's never right to minimize evil! It's never right to side with the sinner against God! We mustn't give strugglers the impression that we are *for* them and God is *against* them! We must make it clear that we are on *God's* side to aid *them*! Let the sinner confess the evil of his evil. If it's needed, *convict* him by confronting him with it. *Don't leave him in his sin without confronting him with it.* There's no greatness so cruel, someone said, as that which leaves a man in his sin.

Don't watch and wait until the struggle becomes a losing one before you step in to help! There aren't many things more detestable than upright people standing by, watching while a struggler becomes increasingly enmeshed in his own folly. They know what is beginning, they know it is destructive, and instead of nipping it in the bud, they allow it to develop and then come down on the sinner like a ton of bricks! This is ungodliness! As soon as you see a fellow pilgrim begin to stumble—*move to the rescue*!

If there's doubt, if you *think* he's in trouble, approach him with real gentleness and with your doubt expressed. Tell him you aren't sure but that you're fearful for him, that you don't want it to go any further if indeed it is happening. Do whatever you need to do to let him know you aren't wanting to bring him needless pain. Tell him he's too precious to you for you to risk *not* approaching him. If you're not that close to him, *talk to someone who is close to him* and tell him of your fears (and doubts, if they exist). This is to ensure that the struggler gets the best chance to take full advantage of the loving confrontation. If he has no very close friends, ask God for help and see him yourself!

Do something about the environment of the struggler if that can be done! We can't live for others. In the end *they* must wrestle with the problems and challenges. Still, we can work to make it easier for them. Is the weekend a tough period for them? Enlist some aid to make those week-ends pleasant and helpful to the struggler. Is their job hindering their life in Christ? Can you help them get another? Do you know anyone who can? Are they intimidated by peers too strong for them? See if you can balance the odds a bit. I'm not saying this very well, but I think you know what I mean.

Give consolation to the struggler. Don't exhort tears from him. Don't *keep on* agreeing with him as he pours out contempt on his evil. Having clearly "sided with God" against the struggler's sin, "side with God" for the sinner. Don't let him feel he is the only sinner in the world, unfit for the company of decent people! Don't act too wise, too forgiving, but do console him!

O Thou who art of purer eyes than to behold iniquity, canst thou bear to look on us conscious of our great transgression? Yet hide not thy face from us, for in thy light alone shall we see light.

Forgive us for the sins which crowd into the mind as we realize thy presence; our ungovernable tempers, our shuffling insincerities, the craven fear of our hearts, the pettiness of our spirits, the foul lusts and fatal leanings of our souls. Not for pardon only, but for cleansing, Lord, we pray.

Forgive us we beseech thee, our unconscious sins; things which must be awful to thy sight, of which we yet know nothing. Forgive by giving in fuller measure, the awakening of thy presence, that we may know ourselves and lose all love of sin in the knowledge of what thou art.

Forgive us for the things for which we can never forgive ourselves; those sad pages of our life which some chance wind of memory blows back again with shame; for the moment of cruel passion, the hour beyond recall, the word that went forth to poison and defame, the carelessness that lost our opportunity, the unheeded fading of bright ideals.

Forgive us for the things that others can never forgive; the idle tale, the cruel wrong, the uncharitable condemnation, the unfair judgment, the careless criticism, the irresponsible conduct.

Forgive us for the sins of our holy things; that we have turned the sacred page without a sigh, read the confessions of holy men and women and never joined therein, lived in thy light and never prayed to be forgiven or rendered thee thanksgiving; professed to believe in thee and love thee, yet dared to injure and hate.

Nothing save being born again, nothing but a miracle of grace, can ever be to us forgiveness. Cleanse our hearts, renew our minds, and take not thy Holy Spirit from us. Amen.

W. E. ORCHARD

6

Church Environment

He who does not have the Church as his Mother does not have God as his Father.

AUGUSTINE

God, we pray for thy Church. We remember with love the nurture she gave to our spiritual life in its infancy, the tasks she set for our growing strength, the influence of the devoted hearts she gathers, the steadfast power for good she has exerted. When we compare her with all other human institutions, we rejoice, for there is none like her. But when we judge her by the mind of her Master, we bow in pity and contrition. Oh, baptize her afresh in the life-giving spirit of Jesus! Grant her a new birth, though it be with the travail of repentance and humiliation. Bestow upon her a swifter compassion with suffering and an utter loyalty to the will of God. Put on her lips the ancient Gospel of her Lord. Help her to proclaim boldly the coming of the Kingdom of God and the doom of all that resist it. Fill her with the prophet's scorn of tyranny and with a Christ-like tenderness for the heavy-laden and down-trodden. Give her faith to espouse the cause of the people, and in their hands that grope after freedom and light to recognize the bleeding hands of the Christ. Bid her cease from seeking her own life, lest she lose it. Make her valiant to give up her life to humanity that like her crucified Lord she may mount by the path of the cross to a higher glory. Amen.

WALTER RAUSCHENBUSCH

The Church of Christ must offer the same salvation to the world that it offers to itself. To do otherwise is to do less than Christ. To do otherwise is to be other than Christ's Body. To do otherwise is to exercise a commission Christ never gave.

LESSLIE NEWBIGIN

The People With The Power To See It Through Have a Healthy . . .

Church Environment

There's no doubt that what Buttrick says is true. It's easier to believe in God than in the church. And the reasons aren't hard to find. *The church is worldly!* Ingersoll's cynical remark scores: "The church has always been willing to swap off treasures in heaven for cash down." And you don't have to be an atheist to know churches are in love with numbers, prestige and praise.

The church is gutless! We don't need concrete illustrations of this. Down through the centuries the church has shown it will take care of itself, come what may. When people needed a prophetic voice, the church was silent or muttered under its breath so it wouldn't be heard. It knows how to "save its own life" and to give good reasons why it should.

The church is blind! When all around her the human race is being trodden under, she majors in pitiable minors.

Narrow issues are her main concern while vast needs stare her right in the face.

The church is divided! New lists of fundamentals are being drawn up every month; circles are becoming more numerous and smaller at the same time. The world titters and is amused for a while at the seriousness with which these "defenders of the truth" brawl in defense of trivia and then with a yawn passes her by. All this Buttrick rightly reminds us of.

But that's only part of the story, says George Arthur, because down the generations there have been thousands of brave, devoted followers of Christ, who have lived and died for the honorable unity of all believers in Christ. And they have been well aware of the big issues as they served God by serving people. Whatever the western nations think of the church, totalitarian nations have feared her. It's with good reason they have tried to suppress her and kill her influence. For she gathers around her men and women of purity and selflessness and *power*! Powerful *as a result* of their devotion to the sinless Christ whose Father is God.

Of course she is unworthy; she's made up of unworthy people and exists *for* unworthy people. (Wasn't it Celsus who made this her badge of shame, that she reached out for and took in all the riff-raff?) *Of course* when compared with him she is shabby at best and vile at worst! But who arms the critics? Who teaches them how to criticize her? She does it herself! In proclaiming Christ she exposes her own stains. If she didn't keep her glorious Master before the eyes of the world, they would have no basis on which to critique her! When they criticize her they are telling her she is not like her Master. Precisely! But if she has managed to give the world a vision of the glorious Christ, then she hasn't totally failed, has she?! That's why, when she is unfavorably compared with her Master, she is sad and glad. Sad that she doesn't measure up better, glad that at least the world knows about his greater glory!

Who criticizes her most, she or outsiders? Have you every heard politicians critique themselves as she does? Do political parties beat their breasts and ask forgiveness, confessing that they made the blunders which economically crushed countless families? Do unions and union bosses confess that the failure to bring about reconciliation with the management is their fault and ask forgiveness? Do outsiders think she's bad? Sure, but nobody scathes her as unsparingly as she does.

But if she's so bad, how does she survive? She survives because the Spirit of the living Lord dwells within her. His deathless life is her life. She is the sign of the reign of God in Jesus Christ! She lives by a power not her own. If she's so bad, why don't we get rid of her? We can't get rid of her! Not only because she is of God, but because we cannot live without her.

We Need the Church Because Her Faith Is Stronger And More Consistent Than Ours

That isn't surprising, is it? Ecclesiastes 4:9-12 is telling the truth. We all know moments of weakness and wandering. We all know how our enthusiasm rises and falls. In the words of Luther: Some days I believe, some days I doubt! We sense our own humanness. If it were left to us alone to promote the good, evangelize the lost, minister to the needy, we'd soon grow weary and suffer from compassion fatigue. Then the work would "go to the dogs."

But she gathers around her and in a fellowship, a grand army of people who, on the whole, are able to keep going. She meanders less than an individual; her strength is greater and her witness for God is more consistent than that of any individual. As a Body she keeps the prayers going heavenward when individuals are empty and prayerless. And because she is more consistent and has more strength, we as individuals are nurtured by that consistent power through the sore years we all experience. Individual faces come and go, some very familiar faces vanish either in apostasy or world-weariness, but she remains!

We Need Her Because Her Traditions and Rites Give Us Security and Perspective

Traditions are only bad when they're bad! The New Testament knows of *good* tradition (2 Thess. 2:15; 3:6). Good things that are passed down from earlier generations suggest stability to us. Religious movements that are brand new are hindered by the very fact that they have no established rites or history. The quest for newness and the derisive dismissal of anything traditional takes its toll. Good traditions bind people together. An established ritual (the word *ritual* doesn't always suggest something bad) gives those involved in it a sense of permanence, security and stability.

As often as we can do (which is very often), Ethel and I go through a daily ritual. I like to jog three or four miles each afternoon about five o'clock. Then I'll soak for about twenty minutes while Ethel makes supper for the two of us. Our kitchen is directly below our bathroom, and Ethel likes to sing while she is making the supper. So not only do I enjoy getting the aches in my body soothed, I get my heart soothed too.

When I come down I set the card table up in front of the fire, put a little tablecloth on it, set out the dishes and we eat together as we watch one of the old movies (you know, the kind they *used* to make). It's such a lovely ritual, filled with warmth, pleasure, mutual gratitude, and it knits us together. It creates a bond, it creates an atmosphere which neither of us can bear to miss. When I'm traveling and it comes around five o'clock, my mind goes to our cheerful fire, the smiles and the togetherness. It's these kinds of traditions, rituals that help keep people together, that bind them with loving cords not easily broken, however strong the pressures that assault the relationship. Families should have loving rituals, joy-bringing rituals, established traditions.

There really *is* great power in great traditions and rituals. We see this in schools, colleges, universities, armies, commercial companies, weight-loss institutions, ball clubs, churches, tribes, families and even (maybe especially) in nations.

Walter Bowie made this very useful observation on circumcision:

> It was the mark which made a man belong to the whole body of the nation whose dignity and consequence he shared thereby. . . . through it a man's life was linked with a great fellowship whose dignity was its high consciousness that it must fulfill the purposes of God. Thus a rite like circumcision can be a vast power for good. It brings the individual into the magnetic field of suggestions and influences greater and more signficant than his lonely self.

This is absolutely true! We find this truth expressed in Israel's whole worship system. George E. Wright rightly reminds us that a central part of Israelite worship was *rehearsal*! Everything was geared to remind them of their roots! Their history was embodied in song! Their public worship involved great confessions which every Israelite had to willingly express. I think you can see this especially clearly in the case of the *firstfruits* offering. There was a national offering and then there were individual offerings. When an individual came to offer his firstfruits, here's what happened (Deut. 26:2-10). He brought a basket of fruit and the priest took it from him, set it before the burnt-offering altar, turned to the offerer and listened while the man rehearsed:

> A wandering Aramean was my father; and he went down into Egypt and sojourned there, few in number; and there he became a nation, great, mighty, and populous. And the Egyptians treated us harshly, and afflicted us, and laid upon us hard bondage. Then we cried to the Lord the God of our fathers, and the Lord heard our voice, and saw our affliction, our toil and our oppression; and the Lord brought us out of Egypt with a mighty hand and an outstretched arm, with great terror, with signs and wonders; and he brought us into this place and gave us this land, a land flowing with milk and honey. And behold, now I bring the first of the fruit of the ground which thou, O Lord, hast given me.

Imagine the sense of togetherness and camaraderie such rituals would inspire! The sense of common roots, common faith. And since the ritual was national and not merely individual, the faith was made stronger. To believe alone is wonderful; to believe *together* is more powerful. Any ritual or tradition which powerfully reminds people of their fellowship, of their purpose for existing is of inestimable benefit to that people. Among other things, the unbroken existence of a tradition or ritual suggests the rightness of the system or (think of July 4th in the U.S.A.) movement connected with that tradition.

There are two rites intimately associated with the church in the New Testament. Baptism and the Lord's Supper (Holy Communion). In the New Testament when people asked what they must do to be saved, they were taught to trustingly and penitently be baptized into union with the blessed Savior, the Lord Jesus Christ (Gal. 3:26-27; Acts 2:36-41).

And those who had in this way taken upon themselves the name of Jesus Christ as Lord, would meet together to eat a simple meal in remembrance of him who had died, been raised and was coming again (1 Cor. 10:14-22; 11:20-29; Acts 20:7).

In both of these loving rites, the central truths upon which the Christian's faith rests are proclaimed. They cry the message that God has demonstrated his love for the world in Jesus Christ who was alive, became dead and was raised to die no more (Rom. 6:3-10; 1 Cor. 11). These ordinances have been committed to the church, in part, that the world might be reminded that God has redemptively acted in the person of Jesus Christ to reconcile the world to himself. These are visible "marks" that we have been chosen by God not only as redeemed people but as the Body through which he goes on heralding and applying the redemption that is in Jesus Christ! *And since we all participate in these ordinances, they mark us out not only as belonging to God, they remind us that we belong to one another (1 Cor. 12:13; 10:17).*

We Need Her Because Her Assemblies Are a Source of Strength to Us

Paul Scherer said this: "A Roman Catholic author is on record as having expressed the opinion that if ever Protestantism should be found dead of an assassin's wound, the dagger in its back would be the Protestant sermon."

Lousy sermons, lousy in content, in relevance, in research and in presentation are part of the reason people don't go to church! Say what you will, even good-hearted people get sick and tired of hearing "one more time" the same worn-out illustrations, clichés, denunciations and someone *fervently* proclaiming *trivia*! As Fosdick would have it: "Only preachers continue to think that people come to church to find out what happened to the Jebusites." (*Leadership has a serious responsibility here!*)

Lots of people won't come to church assemblies because of the dishonorable lives of some church-going people they know. Yes, I know there isn't much sense in that! "My doctor is a silly duffer, so I'm no longer interested in good health." How about: "My next door neighbor butchers Beethoven, so I'm through with good music!"? There's not much sense in that, is there? Everybody knows of someone who has run off with the secretary or the collection (so it would appear), but that doesn't mean Christ isn't real or that his followers are all like that.

You've heard the Ghandi experience, haven't you?! He was a rising young lawyer in Bombay when he heard of the terrible treatment of laborers in South Africa. He decided to go there and plead for them in the courts. One Sunday evening he went to a church and was met at the door by a white-faced, black-hearted member who snarled: "This church isn't open to niggers!" Ghandi swore he would never again enter a Christian assembly. I believe he kept his word. (*Leadership has a serious responsibility here!*)

Many never go to church because they don't want to submit their lives to Christ and they know that that's what they'll be called to do if they assemble.

Some won't come because they feel the churches are unfriendly and have cliques. There are times when this is the sad truth, but we mustn't put too much weight on the assemblies; they are asked to accomplish things that assemblies are not geared to accomplish. You can't get to know *everyone* in an assembly of any size. The assembly is no substitute for being in one another's homes, spending time together at parks, movies, picnics and so forth. You can't establish friendships by merely going to the same assembly week after week. That's asking of the assembly period what it can't possibly do. Don't damn the assembly for something you need to do outside it.

But millions continue to assemble, week after week, without fail, all of their lives. Some go for poor reasons (to please a girlfriend or boyfriend, to establish business contacts, and the like), but millions go for profoundly satisfying reasons. And since they do, *leadership must see to it that they are "fed."* Most people come for the best of reasons.

Seeking Inspiration and Challenge

People go to church seeking inspiration and challenge! Most of the people I know up close feel they lack drive for God. They want the breath of God to fill the flapping sails of their lives and carry them far in devotion and the doing of costly things for God. The endless sermons on "why we are right and everyone else is wrong" just don't cut it! You can only exult in that for so long (if at all).

Katherine Mansfield was a brilliant short story writer, a New Zealand girl who died in France of tuberculosis at the age of thirty-four. Not long before she died some of her friends found her crying. Why? they asked. "It's my stories," said she. "They're no good. I couldn't show a one of them to God!" That's how most sensitive believers feel about their lives of service to God, and they long for someone to lift them above themselves.

And while there's a *real* need for warm sympathy, the sufferers don't want endless pity! They want their eyes lifted up to God and off themselves. They want to be moved to involve themselves in the lives of others. They want new vision! Do you know what the Hebrew writer said to his suffering brothers and sisters? He said: "You have not had to shed blood yet in the struggle against sin!" (Heb. 12:4; Moffatt). The Hebrew writer knows how to sympathize (read the book), but he also knew how to challenge and to inspire (see chapter 11).

Lord Byron wrote an extended poem about the *Prisoner of Chillon*. (It was about an historical character, but it had much more poetry than truth.) Imagine this prisoner, year after year, says Gossip, in a gloomy cell. No companions but those of the insect world with whom the prisoner has made friends. No conversation from his jailers—food shoved at him under the door. High in the prison wall is a single window. One day, after many years in confinement, just to satisfy a whim, he climbs to the window. Exhausted by the effort, with only enough strength to hang on for a few seconds, his wide eyes looked on a blue lake shimmering in the sun. On the far bank, beautiful green hills and a row of neat, lovely little houses. One of them is either his own or something like his own. Birds wheel and talk to one another in the free air as they skim the surface of the lake. His strength is now gone, and he slithers, falls, scrambles back down into the darkness of his cell which has now become a coffin, choking him, suffocating him! Now after years of solitary contentment, he beats against the door of his crypt and cries: "Ah, God, I've got to get out of here! Got to get out! Got to get out of here!"

The people with the power to see it through are confronted with the God who manifested himself on a murderous tree in Palestine! The messages they hear bring them back again and again to the implication of these foundational redemptive acts of God in Christ. Forgiveness is always proclaimed, but the *challenge* of the cross is preached as well as the atoning aspect of it. The gallantry and bravery of the cross is thrust before the heart of people who don't want their religion to be "opium" by which they are put to sleep. They don't want lullabied into a bland decency by "cheap grace" because they realize better than many church leaders, that that is the way of death.

Back in the days when the big ships had sails, it wasn't the balmy nights and sun-drenched beaches the sailors talked about. Home from a two-year trip to the far-flung parts of the world, the sailors would gather round them the village and farm boys. They'd talk of hurricane winds and mountainous waves, of torn sails and broken masts, of driving rain and typhoons, of becalmed days and hot suns baking men's brains. And farm boys in their bare feet would drop their seed bags and run off to sea with a gleam in their eye. Big-bellied shop owners would proudly show the dollars they had made while their childhood friends had been off "wasting their time on pointless and profitless trips" to godforsaken shores. But there was no light in their eyes and no knowledge of having seen visions! And the people with the power to see it through want more than some rotting, mouldy trinkets in their hands as they come before God. "Something for thee!" they want to say as they approach him one day! And healthy assemblies urge them on in that kind of quest.

Coming to Praise and Say "Thank You"

I saw a movie once (I don't remember its title) in which one of the leading characters played an agnostic. He behaved dishonorably, and it resulted in the death of one he loved. Knowing that she was gone beyond his reach and feeling an awful burden of guilt, he said to a friend: "I wish Somebody existed to whom I could say, 'I'm sorry!' "

And I immediately thought of how many deep-seated

needs we have as people. One of them is to say, "Thank you," to someone. When you've read a good book or seen a really fine movie or heard a moving piece of music, haven't you wanted to express your joy by sharing it with someone? Have you never experienced such joy in life—joy that you knew you didn't create—that you wanted to say, *"Thank you,"* to someone?

That's what sensitive people go to church for! They want to praise God and say, "Thank you," to him for all that he has done for them. The joy they feel isn't completed unless they express the fullness of their hearts. (That's part of the reason God calls us to praise him!)

Lots of people have hard lives! And in reading these remarks they're prompted to say they have nothing to be thankful for. But is it true? *Nothing* at all? No health, no warm house to shelter you from the cold? No clean water to drink, no warm food to eat? No friends to weep with or smile with, *no one* to tell your troubles to? No children who love and respect you? No marriage partner to go through life with? No lovely grandchildren to create memories for you when you're old? *Nothing at all?*

No one to whom to sing, "Father of mercies, day by day my love to thee grows more and more"? No one you can sing, "Fairest Lord Jesus, ruler of all nature" to? No reasons to sing, "Love lifted me"? This opportunity is for everyone! Everyone without exception! And this is why people go to church. They can't live without saying, *"Thank you,"* to him whose gifts are strewn along the way like sands upon the great seashore.

People go to church to say, *"Thank you,"* to God because they know they aren't self-made people. It's almost humorous to hear men call themselves "self-made." Men of wealth, fame and acclaim are especially tempted to do this, but you can hear it in every stratum of society.

Take the "self-made" farmer who depends on the soil,

the rain, the sun, the living seed and the seasons for his abundant crops. He didn't build his tractors or create his farm animals. He depends on hired hands (and family, maybe) to harvest the crops. He depends on the public to buy them. Apart from all this, he's a "self-made" farmer.

Take the "self-made" business tycoon. He flies in airplanes he didn't build and can't fly, he uses a telephone he didn't make, holds his business together with computers he didn't create (and probably can't operate), enjoys the free enterprise system he inherited and depends on a mass of other people to cooperate with him in business exchanges. Aside from all that, he's a "self-made" man.

Take the "self-made" philosopher. He was taught at schools he didn't found, read profound books he didn't write, writes with a pen or pencil he couldn't do without or uses a typewriter/word processor he didn't invent, teaches at a school he didn't establish, has his articles accepted by magazines he doesn't own and has his books published by a publishing company he didn't start. Aside from all this, he's a "self-made" philosopher.

Take the "self-made" doctor, dentist, lawyer, butcher, baker, candlestick maker, policeman, airplane pilot, deep-sea diver, schoolteacher, accountant, shorthand secretary. . . . and on and on and on. And do we have *nothing* to be thankful for? *Listen*, people sink below themselves when they refuse to worship someone above themselves! We go to church, thank God, to say, *"Thank you,"* to God!

Coming to Find Conviction and Forgiveness

I *know* churches don't forgive people; I understand that forgiveness isn't found in preachers! But it's at church assemblies that people are consistently confronted with God. And, yes, I understand one can be confronted with God in a multitude of strange places (in a lovely bedroom, in the middle of a rowdy party, in a beer-joint on a mountain hike and so on), but it's at assemblies where God is genuinely praised and his redeeming work is proclaimed by word and rite to the souls of hungry people that we are confronted with God in a consistent and satisfying way.

Those who flock to the church's assemblies don't want to be verbally raped, but they do seek conviction. In the business world there are corners being cut, blacks and whites (which *do* exist) are shaded into grays, sharp practices and income tax evasions are rationalized and people begin to lose perspective. Speech that isn't edifying and a looseness with sacred relationships is encouraged in a world that has no inner reason to act differently. Sensitive believers know all this, feel all this and come looking for renewed perspective. They want to gain *altitude*!

They come looking for truth, decisive truth where God has spoken it. They aren't looking for specific answers to specific questions as much as they're looking for a spirit in which to face these questions. They want to be reminded *whose* they are and *who* they are! They know if they don't find this in church assemblies, they won't find it anywhere! And, though from a purer standpoint, like Ahab they insist that the church maintain its stand for truth no matter how many false voices are trying to please the spirit of the age. (See 1 Kings 22:16 and context.)

The people with the power to see it through don't want their sins whitewashed! While they don't want to be verbally raped, they don't want to be left without a prophetic voice which warns them of the power of the world to press people into its own mold (Rom. 12:2; Phillips). They want to be called from their lethargy and self-centeredness, from the rationalizations concerning brutal and shady business practices they are offered by the world. They want their self-righteousness exposed and the pride of their hearts laid bare. They need to know that in setting themselves above others they are making whatever virtue they have, shabby and worm-eaten at best. There is no kindness so cruel, said someone, as that which leaves a man in his sin without warning him! In later years many will rise up in thankfulness to God for the clear, compassionate, firm voice of the church which speaks God's will for the lives of men.

And they come for forgiveness! Conviction isn't enough; there must be forgiveness. Remember the wise words of Pascal? "It is equally dangerous for man to know God without knowing his own wretchedness, as to know his own wretchedness without knowing the Redeemer who can cure him."

If a man fails to find forgiveness, said E. S. Jones, he fails in the most fundamental area of his life. They come in their multitudes to our assemblies already burdened with a sense of sin and moral failure, and they cannot go on until they know they've been forgiven. And it's there that the sons of comfort and encouragement, the Bible readings about the grace and mercy of God, the prayers of penitent confession bring sinners into direct confrontation with someone who can deal with the Sin problem. And that's what is special about Christ! Others can talk about it, denounce it, expose it, but Christ can *forgive* sin!

He can forgive it *all*. "My sin, O the bliss of this glorious thought, my sin, not in part but the whole, is nailed to the cross and I bear it no more, Praise the Lord, Praise the Lord, O my soul!" First John 1:9 promises that there is an ongoing cleansing of *all* sin for those who walk in the light of God. And God alone knows how much we need that. For sensitive hearts the prayer of John Donne (died 1631) powerfully pleads our heart's crying need:

Wilt thou forgive that sin where I begun,
Which was my sin, though it were done
before?
Wilt thou forgive that sin, through which I
run,
And do run still, though still I do deplore?
When thou hast done, thou hast not
done;
For I have more.

Wilt thou forgive that sin, which I have won
Others to sin, and made my sins their door?
Wilt thou forgive that sin, which I did shun
A year or two, but wallowed in a score?
When thou hast done, thou hast not
done;
For I have more.

I have a sin of fear, that when I've spun
My last thread, I shall perish on the shore;
But swear by thyself, that at my death thy
Son
Shall shine, as he shines now and
heretofore:
And having done that, thou hast done;
I fear no more.

(*A Hymne to God the Father*)

We want *more* than forgiveness, don't you understand! But we want forgiveness! We want what that implies! It implies *life* with God, warmth, fellowship and acceptance. To know that God takes us to his heart and in that honorable way of his, forgives us and calls us his children—this is what we want, old or young, rich or poor, privileged or disadvantaged.

It's been told of "Rabbi" John Duncan that he knew the Hebrew language like his mother tongue. It was rumored that when he prayed he prayed in Hebrew, so some students resolved to listen. Instead of deep theology in the Hebrew tongue they heard the old man say:

Gentle Jesus, meek and mild,
Look upon a little child,
Pity my simplicity,
Suffer me to come to Thee.

They tell the story, too, of Karl Barth (one of the most influential theologians of this century), that when he was asked what the greatest discovery of his whole life was, he answered: "Jesus loves me, this I know, for the Bible tells me so!" I know I've read him saying that his whole literary work can be summed up in one of Paul's phrases: "My grace is sufficient for thee!"

No matter how brilliant, how acclaimed people are, in the final analysis, what they want is their Father. Rudyard Kipling was terribly ill. They thought he would die soon. An old friend of his was watching over him during an especially critical period during that illness. She saw his lips moving and went over to his bed, placing her ear close to his mouth. She heard the old man whisper:

Now I lay me down to sleep,
I pray the Lord my soul to keep,
If I die, before I wake
I pray the Lord my soul to take.

Realizing he wasn't speaking to her she whispered: "I'm sorry Mr. Kipling, I thought you wanted something." The old man said in a little boy's voice: "I do. I want my heavenly Father!"

Some preachers are "fear-mongers." They don't believe in speaking the comfort of sins forgiven. Keep them afraid and they'll work harder, is their approach. It doesn't work and it's ungodly! He was in the mini-bus waiting the return of his friends. The lady begged and begged him to come see her "dancing dogs." She won; he took his friends with him. She led them through her house out to the back. She had some bread with her. Several dogs came running. They were *absolutely* skin and bone. She held the bread just too high for them to get to it, but they were up on their hind legs desperately following the bread wherever she moved it. That's how she kept them dancing so she could earn a few coins! Yes, pathetic, tragic even—but no more pathetic than preachers who keep starving saints "dancing" so they can make a salary or a reputation. The poor woman from Trinidad *may* be excused, but the self-serving preachers? We'll see!

Coming to Find Noble Fellowship

If you love your country and believe in it, says Fosdick, you come away from a high-spirited and patriotic meeting believing in it and loving it more. Of course! And to become part of a patriotic club adds even more to that faith and love. It's no different with Christians. A person who believes in and loves the Christ is helped beyond measure by Christ-centered, high-spirited and noble-intentioned assemblies. They go with their hearts warm and come away fervent; they go with their purpose true and they come away with their true purpose strengthened. That's how God intended it to be. They are helped even more consistently by being part of a congregation of people who, in their social life, are useful, cheerful and God-glorifying. To be in the company of such people (in and out of worship assemblies) is of tremendous help to each disciple.

That's part of the reason John Wesley said: "The Bible knows nothing about a solitary religion!" The Hebrew writer (10:24-25) urges people to provoke one another to love and good works and relates it to the act of assembling together.

Take a look at all of the "one another" passages. In all these the stress is on our oneness, our mutual purpose and faith, our common salvation and our *fellowship*. We are to speak and admonish "one another," to bear "one another's" burdens, pray "one for another," exhort "one another" and comfort "one another." Meetings which stress our unity and oneness in Christ are God's gift to the Community of Faith.

In 2 Timothy 2:22, Paul urges the young man: "Shun the lusts of youth and aim at integrity, faith, love and peace, in the company of those who invoke the Lord out of a pure heart" (Moffatt). Pursue these things "in company with" those who love the Lord. This "in company with" lovers of God, gives us a power which isn't in us as individuals. (All this means that the leadership has a serious responsibility: to see that our assemblies result in edification and to do whatever is required to see that that is accomplished—1 Cor. 14:26.)

It was because she realized the truth in all these things that the lady responded as she did. Here's what happened. Her husband was a hard-drinking man who pushed her around a lot. One Sunday morning as she was getting ready for the assembly, her husband came in from an all-night boozing session.

"And where do you think you're going?" he snarled. She quietly told him she was going to church, and she continued to get dressed. He came over and stuck his face into hers telling her she wasn't going. She acted like she hadn't heard him, so he pushed her up against the wall and yelled at her that she wasn't going to church. When he let her go she just went on getting ready.

He stomped over to the dresser, pulled out a loaded revolver, cocked the hammer and held it to her head. "And what are you going to do now?" the drunken clod said. Quietly and without a trace of fear she said: "If you pull that trigger, I'm going to heaven. If you don't, I'm going to church!" Oh, I love that! Don't you?! We're so tempted to dismiss the fellowship of other Christians and to scorn the notion of assembling. She knew better. We're so easily put off from going (for some of us it takes precious little indeed), but she couldn't be.

To Be Reminded of Our Global Mission

The church is not an end in itself! It is a means to an end also. God has always wanted to bless *all* nations in all ages. Noah, Abraham, Moses and Israel were all called to be blessed but also to *be* a blessing to everyone else. The covenant with Abraham is never mentioned without the global blessing being mentioned. Israel was created a *servant* nation that God's blessings might be brought to the entire world (Is. 49:6). Christ himself was sent to bless the whole world (Jn. 3:16-17). The church is called to that work also!

The "kingdom" of God is the reign of God! And the reign of God, for his own glory and the eternal welfare of his whole creation, is made visible in numerous events and institutions. For example, the Exodus from Egypt was a demonstration of the reign of God in the world. (Think of other events which are like this.) Israel the nation was another witness to the world that God was reigning and wanting to bless it. In the public ministry of Jesus Christ the reign (kingdom) of God comes near. Then God sets him at his own right hand, to reign over all (Eph. 1:20-23).

Jesus left the world and left behind him another Body (the church), through which he ongoingly seeks the redemption of the world. The church, like Israel, is *a sign of the kingdom*! The church is the visible witness that God in Jesus Christ reigns over the world and seeks the blessing and redemption of the world on the basis of the love of God shown in the finished work of Jesus Christ!

The church lives because he lives! The life of the

church is the life he gives her! In her ordinances and in her conduct she proclaims that Christ is Lord of all! She is the sign of the kingdom, the ongoing witness that Jesus is indeed alive and well. Her role is to call the world to see the risen Lord working in her for the world's blessing. She isn't blessed for herself! She is blessed to *be* a blessing. (See Gen. 12:2.) When she seeks only her own blessedness, she is being treacherous!

Newbigin reminds us that the church "found itself surrounded by many religious societies which claimed to offer personal salvation to their members. . . ." This is not the place of the church in the world today. Saints are well-fed while living in a starving world. The church of God if indeed it is to *be* the church of God must be a "church for others." Clearly this means, says Newbigin, "a church which does not exist for itself or for what it can offer its members; a church which is not offering personal salvation to its members apart from the salvation which God offers to the whole world . . . It means a church which is the credible sign of the *malkuth yahweh*, the just and loving rule of God over his whole creation and his whole family."

Assemblies which comfort the afflicted and call them at the same time to remember their mission in the world are a boon to our souls! For leaders to allow the church to drift along serving itself, endlessly feeding itself with the "goodies" of the gospel while the world God so loves is left with ribs showing, is a crime. Such a church is not the church *of Christ*! Such a self-centered community is not the church *of God*! It is the mission of the church, by its life and proclamation, to confront the world with the Lord God who loves them and wishes to bless them. To fail to function in that role is to deny our very reason for existence! Those with the power to see it through are those who are blessed by being part of a congregation which has this truth ever before them!

Peter assures us that the prophets searched intently to find out more about the salvation they were proclaiming (1 Pet. 1:10-12). The one thing they learned for sure was this: "They were not serving themselves but you." The prophets were told: "This good news isn't for you. Others will reap the benefits of your work." This truth needs to be applied anew to the people of God's church today. *Surely it's past time!*

We thank thee, Father, for our place in the Beloved Community which makes its way through the world to become the Eternal City, which even now she is. Bless her increasingly with the heart of Him who so loved her that he gave his life for her. And as she journeys to her final blessing, joy and service in thy presence, grant that she may, in his name, make this world a better place for all to live in.

But there has come to us the awful fear that we could have no place in the Eternal City because of our hostile spirits, our trivial souls, our petty ways. Heaven could never lie around us while hell burns in our hearts. And yet we cannot be content to take our place with those who miss the gate and wander in the outer darkness, homeless and hardening in hate.

Our only hope, O Holy One, is in thy willingness to dwell with us until we are fit to dwell with thee, thou only City of the soul. Amen.

W. E. ORCHARD

Appendix

Before I leave this particular area, let me say a word or two about the prayer-life of the church. I suppose prayer is bragged on more and regarded less than any aspect of Christian living. Most of the time we talk about prayer in the way we think we *should* talk about it. In practice, "sweet hour" of prayer is significantly less than an "hour." I know there are lots of reasons for this, and some of them bear serious examination so that we can grow in prayerfulness.

For many churches, especially those who abhor written creeds and "set prayers," corporate or church prayer is virtually non-existent. Public prayer is often framed in such individual terms and is so concerned with individual needs that the sense of unity and corporateness is lost. (I fully recognize that this doesn't need to be the case. I'm speaking only of what so often happens in practice.)

The Lord's prayer (see Mt. 6:9-13; Lk. 11:2-4) is a model prayer. It wasn't intended to be the only verbal form of prayer, and early Christians used it with latitude. But it was intended to be a *church* prayer, not an individual's prayer! It stresses the oneness of believers, their mutual faith. It isn't, "Give *me* bread for each day, forgive *me* my trespasses, lead *me* not into temptation but deliver *me* from evil (or the evil one)." It is, "*Our* Father, *our* bread, *our* forgiveness, and *our* deliverance from the evil (one)."

To be part of an assembly of people which *together* pours out such a prayer to God is a moving experience indeed. It isn't only right—it is moving! Inspiring! To hear the voice of the congregation *as a congregation,* magnify God, his name, his will, his reign (kingdom) is edifying worship! To hear them, as a body, petition God on behalf of the whole Body that He might give, forgive, lead and deliver, is strengthening.

Set prayers have their dangers, traditional prayers can become mere ritual, but there's also the danger that the worship of the church can become the property of a handful of ministers. There's the danger that the extemporary prayers of individuals who are called to "lead in prayer" will remain forever shallow and that "congregational" prayer will become tiresome, common and repetitious. Something to be gotten out of the way so we can get to the central issue—the preaching.

One of the central elements in congregational worship in the New Testament was prayer (Acts 2:42, *the* prayers). Speaking of congregational prayer, in early church history, Everett Ferguson remarks: "The prayers preserved a strong sense of the community, of life in the church, in which the welfare of all was bound together. Thus Christians prayed together, and prayed '*our* Father.' Prayer was the property of the whole people of God."

It's clear from the New Testament (and early church history) that individual prayer was an important part of the disciple's life. It isn't difficult to locate a dozen books written on that, books urging us to grow in the area of personal prayer. This is good!

It seems to me we need to do something about our congregational prayer. Song-leaders are chosen to help organize and guide our worship in song. This is great! Teachers and preachers are chosen to guide our study, and this is right! Our congregational prayer is left to the "one appointed" five minutes beforehand. Public (not to mention private) prayer is not taken seriously. Prayer time should be given as much serious thought as preaching/teaching time.

7

Assurance In the Godhead

Hear O Israel, the Lord our God is one Lord!

DEUTERONOMY 6:4

When earth's lights are fading and stricken men call;
To say less than God is to say nothing at all.
Man's ultimate hour cries for ultimate power:
Only God is enough!

SELECTED

No man has ever seen God, but God the One and Only, who is at the Father's side, has made him known.

JOHN 1:18

After hearing the story of what God has done and was doing in Jesus Christ, a Chinese gentleman jumped to his feet and joyously shouted at his wife: "Didn't I tell you? There ***had*** *to be a God like that!"*

E. S. JONES

For we must all appear before the judgment seat of Christ, that each one may receive what is due him for the things done while in the body, whether good or bad.

2 CORINTHIANS 5:10

If ever God was man or man was God, Jesus Christ was both.

BYRON

In the same way, the Spirit helps us in our weakness. We do not know what we ought to pray, but the Spirit himself intercedes for us. . . .

ROMANS 8:26

The People With
The Power To See It Through
Have . . .

A God Fit To Worship

Because God has manifested himself in Jesus Christ, we know what he is like. I don't mean we know *everything* about him—that isn't possible for us. Even Jesus Christ couldn't *exhaustively* show us God since God is too majestic and grand to be fully manifested in human form. But what we have seen of God in Jesus Christ is truly what God is like (Jn. 1:18; 14:6-10; Col. 1:15).

And once you've met him, once you've truly met him and know you've met him, you know him forever because he doesn't change (Heb. 13:8). So the good news is, there is one God and he is forever like Jesus Christ! And *that* can give you the power to see it through!

And God is fit to worship!

In a world full of gods, adored and served by zealous worshipers, we see enough to sicken and sadden us. There are an endless number of cults proclaiming the deity of their gods. *Health* is worshiped, *education* is worshiped, *science* is worshiped, *power* is worshiped, *money* is worshiped, *pleasure* is worshiped, *race* is worshiped, *nationalism* is worshiped, *music* is worshiped, and so is the *family*. All of these, ultimately, are forms of worships of the grand god of gods: *self*. Many thoughtful observers of mankind are calling this the "age of Narcissus." (Greek mythology tells us of a young man in Greece who fell in love with his own image in the water. Every time he reached in to touch the water-nymph it vanished in the ripples. He lay there until he died, smitten with love for his own reflection. On that spot there grew up a flower called the Narcissus.)

If we make these things *servants* and sanctify them by offering them to God in service to our fellow-humans, they're fine. To make them *gods* is perdition! None of them is *big* enough to worship. *Man cannot find within Man or the joys of Man the reason for his existence!* Family and health and music are all very well, but they're too small. They lack power, depth and permanence to satisfy what is placed in us by God! Wasn't it Augustine who said that we were made for God and our hearts are restless until we are at home with him?

In Spielberg's *E.T.* the extraterrestrial is befriended by earth children who feed, protect and care for him. They give him all they have to give and they give it lovingly, but when they ask him where his home is, he points sadly into the sky and mournfully says: "Home!" And throughout the movie, with sad eyes and sad voice he tells them of his loneliness and homesickness. What they gladly gave him wasn't enough! There was something they *couldn't* satisfy no matter how they wished they could!

It's the same with us! We're too well created to live by bread alone! We're too richly endowed to be satisfied with mere music or degrees or acclaim (no matter how wonderful or worthwhile). We won't be satisfied until we know as we are known, until we discover our destiny the *ultimate* reason we are alive. *Only God is enough!*

Only God is big enough to make sense out of so much that appears senseless (and may be forever, in itself, senseless)! Only God is rich and deep enough to fill our eternal longings to the full. Will he make the light and not make the eye? Will he make the music and not make the ear? Will he make the food and not make the palate. Will he fill us with deep, unutterable longings (which we feel in our better moments) and not provide the ultimate fulfillment? *God is fit to worship because he's big enough!*

And listen, since we've met him in Jesus Christ, his character doesn't surprise us. In one way, the character of Jesus Christ *should* have been predictable! The Creator is greater than the creature. That makes sense. But not just greater in power because raw power is a poor criterion by which to judge greatness. (We're all acquainted with the power-wielders like Ghengis Khan, Attila, Hitler, Napoleon and Stalin. Or on a lowlier level, but of the same kind—the school bully! We don't think they're so great. In fact, we don't think they're great at all!)

No, we judge greatness by the *virtue* possessed (another kind of power altogether). Have we seen exhibitions of selflessness which took our breath away? Yes! If God couldn't match that, the creature would be greater than the Creator. Haven't we read of or come across people who suffered beyond measure that others might be blessed. If God couldn't match that then the creature would leave his Creator behind. When we see the pained compassion of even God's critics (like Somerset Maugham or Thomas Hardy) as they agonize over the hurt of people, are we to conclude that the admirable compassion and empathy is in the creature but absent in the Creator? No, the world that contains cancer, cholera, hunger and loneliness is the same world that has hearts like God and . . . Jesus Christ! When the world's lovely people are moved to act against those things which torment mankind they are acting out their Creator's feelings! *Nobody "out-feels," "out-serves" or "out-suffers" God!* We rightly think people of nobility and selflessness are worthy of our praise and esteem. It's for that reason God is supremely fit to be worshiped!

In Browning's marvelous poem *Saul*, David is greeted by his brother Abner at Saul's tent. He tells the boy that the king is wrestling in the darkness with death but has asked for him. David finds his way into the blackness of the tent and there finds Saul, standing against the central post of the tent with his arms stretched out on the cross beam, a figure "blackest of all." David begins to sing, and Saul slowly begins to move back from the brink of death but for all his singing he cannot bring him fully into life. He sings of Saul's fame and status, of *anything* he can think of to make the king think life is worthwhile.

And while David agonizes, wishing, even at the cost of taking his own life, to give endless life to the king, "the truth" comes upon him. If he, a sinful man, loved Saul so much, God loved him more! David would become poor to make Saul rich; he would starve to give Saul bread—would God? "Would I," says David, "in my impotent yearning do all for this man, And dare doubt he alone shall not help him, who yet alone can?" The creature, David concludes, can't "surpass the Creator." *Think noble things of God!*

O Thou who art the Father of that Son which hast awakened us and still urges us out of the sleep of our sins, and exhorteth us that we become thine, to thee, Lord, we pray, who art the supreme Truth, for all truth that is, is from thee. Thee we implore, O Lord, who art the highest Wisdom, through thee are wise, all those that are so. Thou art the supreme Joy, and from thee all have become happy that are so. Thou art the highest Good and from thee all beauty springs. Thou art the intellectual Light and from thee man derives his understandings. To thee, O God, we call and speak. Hear us, O Lord for thou art our God and our Lord, our Father and our Creator, our Ruler and our Hope, our Wealth and our Honor, our Home, our Country, our Salvation, and our Life; hear, hear us, O Lord. Few of thy servants comprehend thee, but at least we love thee—yea, love thee above all other things. We seek thee, we follow thee, we are ready to serve thee; under thy power we desire to abide, for thou art the Sovereign of all. We pray thee to command us as thou wilt; through Jesus Christ thy Son our Lord. Amen.

KING ALFRED, 849

The People With The Power To See It Through Have . . .

A Lord Worth Serving And Following

It was the poet Byron who said: "If ever God was man or man was God, Jesus Christ was both!" Here and there you come across someone who thinks Jesus Christ was quite ordinary, but such people are rare indeed. In a literary gathering one of the gentlemen read some of Shelley's writings. Everyone was duly appreciative of what the poet had to say. The reader then remarked: "I met a man the other day who thought there was nothing much to Shelley. Poor devil!" Enough said!

It isn't just that millions look to Jesus for the forgiveness of sins and the way to the Father; it isn't simply that he is the Ransom for sinful mankind and the coming Judge of humanity; it isn't just that without him there we cannot enter the presence of the holy God that draws his followers to Christ. It *is* these things, but there's more to it than that!

It's his attractiveness! His nobility, his bravery, gentleness, kindness, honesty and loyalty. The very thought that such a thoroughly fearless Man will kneel in prayer, confessing need, drives from us our sinful embarrassment which tempts us to avoid such "religious" and "weak" habits that wise philosophers like Kant would smile at. The thought that sophisticated people would look at each other in well-mannered amusement if they saw us pray or hear us say that we prayed—such a thought often keeps people from praying or speaking of it as their habit. But a vision of Jesus, earnestly pouring out his heart to his Father, redeems us from our timidity and protects us from their unspoken derision.

We hide behind him, thank God, in our weakness. When we don't have answers, when the grins of our peers have us rattled, when the sneer of the critic has us trembling, we look toward Christ. And when we are assured *he* has identified himself with us in these words or in that way to behave or in that kind of response, we're cheered and strengthened. Just to know it is like him disarms the enemy and makes our spirits soar again!

I read of a young, unknown artist who sat in a gallery looking rapturously at one of the masterpieces. People came and went, but he sat on for a very long time. After a long time he could contain himself no longer, and with pride and joy on his young face he turned to the handful of people gazing with him at the portrait and unselfconsciously said: "I am an artist too!" I love that story! He felt such pride at such a glorious work by someone who was of his profession, that he was compelled to identify with him.

And so it is with Jesus Christ. We look at him in all his manhood, and the sight fills us with such pride and joy that we are thrilled that we, too, are humans! I mentioned something like this earlier when I told you of

Quiller Couch's compliment to Robert Louis Stevenson. Everyone in England, said Couch, wrote with an eye on a little island in the South Sea where Stevenson was living out his last days. They hoped Stevenson might hear of their work and not think it too unworthy. Just to be in the same profession as Stevenson. Just to be in the same profession as Michelangelo or Bach or da Vinci. *Just to be part of the humanity which includes Jesus Christ of Nazareth!*

And it isn't just his character and general lifestyle that draws people to this noble Knight of God, it's what he undergoes on their behalf that makes him so attractive. His bravely choosing death to rescue mankind from the World Hater and the emptiness of their own lives gives him his drawing power. In his dying he tells us many important things.

In His Cross Christ Tells Us He Thinks We're Worth Dying For!

Who else, knowing mankind as well as he, would tell us such a thing? Seely confessed that the more he grew to know about life and the universe the more pessimistic he grew and the more contemptuous of his fellow man as well as himself he became. Thomas Hardy had no respect for and Freud never spoke well of man. But Jesus thought Man was worth dying for, from the least to the greatest. And it wasn't a grim stubbornness which led him to this view. For all the tears and fears, Christ joyfully chose the cross just to do the will of God in being Man's champion against the forces of evil which would damn him!

In His Cross Christ Intimates That We Will Live Forever!

William Cowper, in closing a letter to a friend, wrote a wonderful thing. He said: "There is not room enough for a friendship such as ours to unfold itself in full bloom in a tiny little life like this. Therefore I am, and must, and will be, Yours for ever." I love that, don't you?! It means that every loving relationship prophesies of a larger life, a wider world, where love can fully develop.

Christ tells us that in the cross! Everyone who has given a moment's thought to it realizes that the love of God expressed to us in Christ's dying for us is too grand, too astonishingly deep, to work itself out fully in a little life like ours. In this life we experience marvelous things from his hand but, for all that, in looking at the cross, we instinctively feel: "All that just for this little life?" This God, says Paul, "He that spared not his own Son, but delivered him up for us all, how shall he not with him also freely give us all things?" (Rom. 8:32; KJV).

A visitor to New York asked the taxi driver what the writing on the building, "The Past is Prologue," meant. The taxi driver thought for a moment and said: "It means, 'You ain't seen anything yet!' " In the cross of Jesus Christ we are told: "This is only the beginning expression of the love of God. There's more to come!"

And the Resurrection Has a Message For Us Too!

The resurrection tells us that evil loses! If the cross had been the end, says Paul in 1 Corinthians 15, Christians would be of all the people in the world most miserable. Evil, no matter how powerful, no matter how entrenched, no matter how deeply rooted—evil loses!

The resurrection tells us that death loses! The graveyard has a powerful voice. The older the graveyard the more powerful its message! Each weather-beaten, barely-legible gravestone preaches that death has had a hold on man for a long time. The pyramids are silent witnesses of the power of death. The city of Death is the largest city in the universe, someone said. Alexander the Great is there. So is Julius Caesar and Nebuchadnezzar. Hitler and Napoleon are there along with all the mightiest names of history (from day *one* until now). But a young man from Galilee is known now to multiplied millions as *The Death Killer*.

Browning in his marvelous *A Death in the Desert* pictures the aged apostle John dying. Pamphylax, Xanthus, Valens and the Boy were trying to make him comfortable. They had been waiting sixty days for him to die. He smiles a little now and then; they try to give him some wine to revive him that he might speak just one more time. They rubbed his hands, massaged him with an ointment/perfume and prayed, but nothing would revive the old man. "Then the Boy sprang up from his knees, and ran, Stung by the splendor of a sudden thought." He read from the plates in the hearing of John, the words: "I am the resurrection and the life." At this John opened his eyes wide, at once, and began to speak one more time! Isn't that marvelous?! And we're assured that this voice that first spoke those words will be the voice which will wake the dead on a coming day and expose Death as the failure it is! *This* is the Lord that those who have the power to see it through have trusted and committed themselves to.

Precious Lord Jesus, for thy love of us which took you so far from home, we humbly thank thee. For being our champion against all who would destroy us, especially we ourselves, we truly praise thee. For believing in us when thy experience of us has been so disappointing we adore thee. For the grandeur of thy manhood, the depth of thy earnestness, the purity of thy life, the cheerfulness of thy face, the loyalty of thy heart we worship thee. For all the things about thee that make us humbly grateful to be called thy servants and friends we bow down before you. Amen.

The People With The Power To See It Through Have . . .

A Spirit To Strengthen And Help

I don't have my thinking systematized on *how* the Spirit does a lot of what the New Testament says he does, but I'm not going to let my ignorance deprive me of the comfort that such New Testament teaching brings. If I can't explain a host of the everyday experiences of billions of people, should it surprise me that I don't have a good grasp on the complexities of our interpersonal relationships with the Spirit of God?

I have some definite convictions about what the Spirit of God isn't and what he doesn't do. He isn't a "super bellboy" who provides parking spaces for people who happened to be in a hurry to keep an appointment. I tire of hearing this kind of nonsense! I'm not saying the Spirit of God can't or won't do such a thing! I'm not even saying he hasn't done so, at some time or another; but I resent the third Person of the Godhead being assigned car-park attendant duties by some glib and self-centered person who seems to have him in their pocket!

And it bothers me to hear people make endless claims about the things the Spirit of God says to them. He tells them where to get their hair done, what kind of car to buy, if they ought to vacation in Florida or Colorado and, of course, what certain Scriptures mean (even when what he has "told them" runs contrary to the plain wording of the Scriptures themselves). And I've heard so many people say: "The Spirit led me do this . . ." and what they were "led" to do was so unlike God. To ask such people how they know it is the Spirit of God that's doing all these things is a *no-no*. We're supposed just to take their word for it. You understand, it isn't *the Spirit of God* I doubt!

One lady came to speak to me on some issues about which we disagreed. As soon as she sat down she told me she got her teaching directly from the Holy Spirit and quoted 1 John 4:6 to me: "We are from God, and whoever knows God listens to us; but whoever is not from God does not listen to us. This is how we recognize the Spirit of truth and the spirit of falsehood." In no uncertain fashion she made it clear that there was no room for my disagreeing with her. The problem here is not with the Spirit of God. John I know, Paul I know, Peter and the apostles I know, Jesus I know—but who are these people who have a monopoly on the Spirit's wisdom, revelation and everyday guidance? Let me say it again: It isn't the *Spirit of God* I have doubts about!

One more thing before moving on to look at some biblical texts on the Spirit. Right or wrong, I don't believe the Spirit of God works only in the lives of those who have made Jesus Lord! God told Cyrus in Isaiah 45:5: "I am the Lord, and there is none other; apart from me there is no God. I will strengthen you, though you have not acknowledged me." *If God waited until we became Christians before he helped us, how could we ever become Christians in the first place?* Like Cyrus, we have been blessed and helped by God since we first drew breath (and before!).

Wherever honor and beauty and gallantry are seen, there the Spirit of God has been at work! It's the worst kind of "Christian imperialism" to claim that only Christians can be honorable and brave and lovely in life! *Of course* there are blessings Christians have which the unforgiven don't have, but Christians don't have a monopoly on God's love, blessings and help in the fight against evil!

And it doesn't matter that people don't acknowledge their bravery and compassion as the work of God's Spirit in them; it's true just the same. It didn't matter that Cyrus didn't give God the praise for his victories. It changed nothing that he believed numerous gods gave his power. It is enough that the God of gods tells us that he was behind it all. People don't need to acknowledge that God gives them rain and fruitful seasons, filling their hearts with gladness (Acts 14:17)—it's true just the same.

The Spirit of God is a gift from God! Over and over again in the New Testament we're told that the Holy Spirit is God's gift to his people. In Acts 2:38-39 people were told to penitently be baptized in Christ's name unto the forgiveness of their sins and they would "receive the gift of the Holy Spirit" because the promise was unto everyone without exception!

No one earns a *promise* or a *gift*! God doesn't give the Spirit to people because they've merited it. In Galatians 3:14 and Ephesians 1:13-14, Paul reminds us that the Spirit is "the promised" Spirit. As Canaan was Israel's "promised land" and their "inheritance," so the Spirit is the believer's "promised Spirit" and (the earnest of) his inheritance. The *heir* doesn't earn his inheritance; it's *given* to him!

The Spirit of God gives strength! In Ephesians 3:16, we're told that the Spirit strengthens us with power. In Philippians 1:19, Paul speaks of the "help" the Spirit gives. The Greek word there speaks of an abundant supply.[1] The Holy Spirit is known as the "Comforter" (from *paraklētos*). Wycliffe was the first to so translate it but to him it didn't mean someone who spoke soothingly or tenderly. *Comfort*, to him, meant to make brave, give fortitude to. The Spirit of God not only gives counsel, or advocacy, he gives strength. How does he do that? For the moment that doesn't matter—the *fact* is, he *does* it! (See 1 Pet. 5:10!) (All these passages speak to Christians, but this doesn't mean the Spirit of God doesn't enable and strengthen people who aren't Christians. When Ephesians 5 tells us Christ died for the church, we aren't to conclude he didn't die for the whole of mankind because he did—1 Jn. 2:2.)

The Spirit of God makes us different! That's what the word *holy* means—different! The Spirit *sanctifies* Christians (1 Pet. 1:2): "Who have been chosen according to the foreknowledge of God the Father, through the sanctifying work of the Spirit, for obedience to Jesus Christ and sprinkling by his blood." Involved in the idea of Christian *sanctification* is the central notion that they now *belong to God*. It isn't just that they're different; their difference involves the truth that they are God's!

The Spirit works to *positionally* make Christians into Christians (he positions them in Christ and out of the world). The Spirit continues to work with Christians to *personally and progressively* sanctify them. (See Heb. 12:14 and 1 Pet. 1:2). As soon as a person becomes a Christian he is "set apart" (made holy), and as he continues on in his relationship with Christ, he is molded more and more into the likeness of Christ by the sanctifying work of the Spirit. (How many instruments the Spirit uses in accomplishing his end, the exact *how* of it, and such questions don't matter for the moment. The *fact* of it we need to acknowledge! However he does it, he *does* it! However many are the surgeon's instruments, it is the surgeon who does the surgery. We don't thank the scapel and the scissors when a successful surgery is completed because we know the surgeon did the job! The *Spirit*, in cooperation with the Christian, does the sanctifying!)

The Spirit produces the fruit mentioned in Galatians 5:22-23! We don't have to browbeat the Spirit into doing this kind of work in us! He's eager to mold and make us into the likeness of Christ. Wherever and whenever we see people becoming more and more like Jesus Christ, we are seeing the Spirit of God at work.

If a man is accused of physical cruelty to his family, the *kind* of evidence the court looks for is bruised children and a beaten wife. This is the kind of fruit such a man produces. When you see people acting in ways unlike Jesus Christ, teaches Paul (Gal. 5:19-21), you can be sure they aren't following the guidance of the Spirit. But when you come across those whose lives are increasingly conforming to Christ's image, you are seeing the work of the Spirit in them. The proof of the Spirit at work in them is the fruit they manifest.

Left to himself, man would cheerfully pursue evil to every conceivable depth. It's the grace of God in the work of the Spirit to *every* man (Christian and non-Christian alike) that God keeps a curb on sin! Christ's claim in John 15:5 that apart from him they could do *nothing* was no exaggeration!

The agnostic, Bertrand Russell, was speaking of the apes in the zoo when he spoke of: "the strange, strained sadness in their eyes. One can almost imagine that they feel they ought to become men, but cannot discover the secret of how to do it." He continues this way: "On the road to evolution they have lost their way: their cousins marched on, and they were left behind." Then, poignantly, he says: "Something of that same strain and anguish seems to have entered the soul of civilized man. He knows there is something better than himself almost within his grasp, yet he does not know where to seek it, or how to find it. . . . "

I have nothing to say here to those who *want* nothing better! Some of us want no better because we prefer the self-serving life of "wine, women and song." Others of us want nothing better because we think we have arrived and you can't improve on perfection. Others of us want nothing better because we compare ourselves with those around us and think we look good by comparison.

But to those who feel at times what Russell imagined about apes, the Bible points us to a sure way to increased likeness to God: the work of the Spirit within us! Don't worry about the *how*! He'll do it! Don't worry about the *when*. He'll do it! Simply cooperate and use such strength as he ongoingly gives you and *relax*! Our aim and goal *and* our hope is a radical Christlikeness and we've been assured that God by his Spirit will work that in us (2 Cor. 3:17-18; Eph. 3:14-20).

But if all this is true, if the Spirit of God is there, willing and able to strengthen us, why aren't we better than we now are? Why aren't we much more like Jesus Christ?

I can't really say. Maybe we're underestimating the gap between us and Jesus Christ! Maybe we're not sufficiently aware of how evil we are and how actively (even if sometimes subconsciously) we fight against the changes the Spirit wishes to make in us. Maybe we're fairly happy about the "good" condition we're in at present and aren't vigorously cooperating with the Spirit in his work in us. I don't know where the work of God, the Holy Spirit and our human response to him meet, but I know he is resistible (Acts. 7:51). I'm certain of this: *The problem doesn't lie in the Spirit!* I'm certain of this too: The Spirit of holiness will make us holy through and through. . . . he who called us is faithful and he will do it (1 Thess. 5:23-24).

O Thou plenteous Source of every good and perfect gift, shed abroad the cheering light of thy sevenfold grace over our hearts. Yes, Spirit of love and gentleness, we most humbly implore thy assistance. Thou knowest our faults, our failings, our necessities, the dullness of our understanding, the waywardness of our affections, the perverseness of our will. When, therefore, we neglect to practice our minds, rectify our desires, correct our wanderings, and pardon our omissions, so that by thy guidance we may be preserved from making shipwreck of faith, and keep a good conscience, and may at length be landed safe in the haven of eternal rest; through Jesus Christ our Lord. Amen.

ANSELM, 1033

Endnote

[1]Walter Bauer, *A Greek-English Lexicon of the New Testament and Other Early Christian Literature*, 4th ed. Revised by William F. Arndt and F. Wilbur Gingrich (Chicago, Ill.: University of Chicago Press, 1957), 305.

Bibliography

It isn't difficult to fill several pages with book titles, and it's a temptation ("Wow, what a reader that guy is!"). But most books (and maybe this is one of them) have only a few really worthwhile things to say. On the whole they're poor books, so why inflict them on the poor readers? It isn't the *number* of books read, it's the *quality* that matters. Better to read a few really good books than a warehouse of mediocrity.

Before you buy any of these mentioned, you might want a second opinion from someone you know and respect and who knows you. I loaned a book I prize to a friend not too long ago. He returned it with a shrug. I was surprised at his very low opinion of it, but that's how it goes with people and books. On the other end, I reviewed a book by a popular writer a few years ago and gave it a poor rating. Some friends were almost indignant. So . . . you've been warned! If you don't see a book mentioned that you think is great, it means (1) I haven't read it, (2) I read it and didn't think it great or (3) I read it and thought it was great but forgot to mention it!

Here are a few I think are worth mentioning. Those I think would be difficult reading for the average person will be followed by an asterisk (*).

Berkouwer, G. C. *Sin*. Grand Rapids, Mich.: Wm. B. Eerdmans Publishing Co., 1971.* (In the "Dogmatic" series.)

Mackintosh, H. R. *The Christian Experience of Forgiveness.*

Menninger, Karl. *Whatever Became of Sin?* New York: Hawthorn Books, 1973.

Orr, James. *Sin as a Problem Today.**

Ramm, Bernard. *Offense to Reason: The Theology of Sin*. New York: Harper and Row, 1985. (I found this readable, but read some snatches of it before you buy it just in case.)

Tournier, Paul. *Guilt and Grace*. New York: Harper and Bros., 1962.

Books on suffering:

Bayly, Joseph. *The Last Thing We Talk About* (formerly: *View from a Hearse*). Elgin, Ill.: David Cook Publishing Co., 1973.

Jones, E. Stanley. *Christ and Human Suffering*. New York: Abingdon Press, 1933.

Kushner, Harold S. *When Bad Things Happen to Good People*. New York: Avon, 1963.

Lewis, C. S. *The Problem of Pain*. New York: Macmillan Publishing Co., 1978.

Nouwen, Henri. *The Wounded Healer*. Garden City, N.Y.: Doubleday, 1979.

Stewart, George. *God and Pain*. New York: George Doran, 1927. (A great book but out of print.)

Yancey, Phillip. *Where Is God When It Hurts?* Grand Rapids, Mich.: Zondervan Publishing Co., 1977.

When I'm feeling down on people, Harry E. Fosdick really helps me. He still has a number of books in print (e.g., *As I See Religion, The Meaning of Faith, The Meaning of Prayer, The Meaning of Service*). When I'm down on me, A. J. Gossip gives me a needed lift. He has at least two in print: *From the Edge of the Crowd* (T. & T. Clark) and *The Galilean Accent* (T. & T. Clark). Lewis Smedes wrote a good little book: *How Can It Be All Right When Everything Is All Wrong?* I'm forever helped by a set of books called *The Speaker's Bible* (ed. Edward Hastings, Baker Book House, 18 vols.). Really worth having! Leslie D. Weatherhead's books are full of wonderful stories and useful insights (e.g., *The Will of God, Time for God, A Private House of Prayer, Overcome Fear and Despair, Prescription for Anxiety, The Meaning of the Cross, Life Begins at Death*). Robert Browning's poetry is sometimes absolutely breathtaking (e.g., *A Death in the Desert* or *Saul*). Everyone should be *made* to read the classics (if he *wants* to). Books like *Lorna Doone, Silas Marner, Don Quixote, Les Misérables, The Scarlet Letter, Moby Dick, A Tale of Two Cities* (and on and on) are too rich to be missed. *Friendship Evangelism* by Joseph C. Aldrich is a really fine book! Biographies of great men and women (biblical and extra-biblical) are a rich source of inspiration and strength. The *New International Dictionary of the Christian Church* (Zondervan) is a first rate book. The Inter-Varsity Press has recently published a *New Dictionary of Theology*.* Very good!